Endorsements

Lon Cole is a survivor. He has overcome child abuse, serious wounds on the battlefield, severe depression, post-traumatic stress disorder, heart disease, and brain aneurysms. Now he is living with Alzheimer's disease. No—to say that is to understate Lon's unyielding fortitude and steadfast determination. Rather, he is *living* with Alzheimer's. As he often says, "I have Alzheimer's. Alzheimer's does not have me!"

This book, his third, includes not only his latest poems but also the story of his life. Once again, Lon's words, like his life, are infused with clarity, courage, faith, and love.
The most compelling voices in the fight against Alzheimer's stigma are those of individuals living with the disease, people who are not ashamed of their diagnosis and are willing to share their stories openly—people like Lon. In his poetry, at his book signings, as a member of our Early Stage and Pierce County Regional Advisory Councils, Lon inspires others living with Alzheimer's to be open and direct about their disease, communicate the facts, seek support, stay connected, and, above all, do not be discouraged.

I'm very proud of Lon. He's a valued colleague, dear friend, and valiant champion in our battle against Alzheimer's disease.

Bob Le Roy
Executive Director
Alzheimer's Association Washington State Chapter

Through his wonderful books *"You're Never Alone"* and *"Alive And Thankful"* Lon Cole has brought a unique look at life through his poems.

You now have in his new book *"Celebrate Survival"* an opportunity to follow Lon through his life history up to this point, You now can see the background that will bring you to a closer view and understanding of the creation of his poems. Lon has the ability to view life from an unique vantage point. He then miraculously transfers this view to inspirational and emotional rhyming verse. He takes you to the depths of concern, then to the heights of joy and happiness. His love for life no matter what it contains, is positive, as evident though out all his writings . Enjoy! It's what life is all about. As Lon always tells you "Be alive and thankful"

John M Davis, PhD

TO
Nick
Hang in there

Celebrate
Survival

[signature]

Celebrate
Survival

LON COLE

A&T

A&T PUBLISHING
PUYALLUP, WASHINGTON

Celebrate Survival

ISBN 13:978-0692842553

ISBN 10: 0692842551

A & T Publishing

Puyallup. Washington

aliveandthankful.com

Contents

Celebrate Survival
You Rocked My Life
You're Not on Your Own
You're Not Alone
You're Looking at the Best
WWII Vets
Why We Have Pain
Where Do We Go
When Warriors Get Old
What Joy I Have
What Is a Patriot
We Owe So Much to You

New Year Is Coming
Never Leave You Alone
Never Give It Up
Never
Letting Go
Nature's Wrath
Nature's Battle
Nature Is Beauty
Nature's Resume
My Partner
Music to My Ears
Mother's Day
Mother Nature
Memories of Childhood
Memorial Day
Made in the US of A
Love the Lord
Love Is Eternal
Live to Be Happy
Live to Be Free
Live by the Truth
Listen while You Pray
Listen to the Lord
Lift Others Up
Life Isn't Over When You're Going to Die
Life Is an Adventure
Life Is a Journey
Life Is a Gift
Life Goes On
Life Is a Special Gift
Let the Wind Be on Your Side
Know What's Real
Knowledge Is Freedom
Nature Is a Gift
Live Life Large

Letting Go
Keep Us Safe
Joy Is Always There
Joy in the Journey
It's a New Year
Is There More to Thanksgiving
I Served My Country Well
I Need to Be Free
I'm Haunted with Guilt
I Love the Beach
I'll Never Regret
I Know He Is Free
I Got Swallowed by Horny Toad
Hope Is Near
Hope
Hold to Your Faith
Hold On
He Will Set You Free
He's Now in Heaven
Heroes
He Is Our Hero
A Hard Wooden Floor
Hard to Repent
Halloween
Grandchildren Are a Joy
Good Days
God Only Knows
God Loves Us All
Give Love a Chance
Friends
Free from Pain
Freedom Is a Privilege
Freedom
Forgiveness
Flag of the USA

Fitness
Feel All Alone
Family
Faith, a True Course
Faith and Beyond
Eyes of the Lord
Easter
Each Step We Take
Donuts
Don't Lose Hope
Dementia
Demented
Death and Beyond
Darkness
Creation
Columbus
Cold as Ice
Christmas to Treasure
Christmas Memory
Christmas, a Sacred Day
Celebrate Survival
Carry You So Far
Be on the Right Side
Believe in the Miracle
Be Humble and True
Beauty Surrounds Us
Beach
Be All You Can
A Witness from Above
Autumn or Fall
A Special and Sacred Time
A Special Gift from Above
Arms Open Wide
Anger Is a Feeling
A New Year Will Start

A New Year Comes
A Medic's Call
Alive and Thankful
A Great Journey
A Family with Love
Without Reward
A Brighter Day
Nine/Eleven

Foreword

I'll never forget the feel of bullets whizzing by me. Many times, I've wished to forget seeing a middle school boy shot over a bowl of rice. I'll probably never forget the mass graves of rubble that covered Port-au-Prince after the disastrous 2010 earthquake. I can't forget the smell of death. Every day was about survival while I worked in Haiti as a photojournalist and later as a relief worker. I don't know that I knew then how to celebrate survival.

Lon's story of survival has intrigued me since we met at the Alzheimer's Association. He's the first person I've met who always greets folks with a booming voice, "I'm alive and thankful! How are you?" I've often wondered how he could be so joyful while fighting Alzheimer's disease and lingering PTSD symptoms from the Vietnam War.

In his memoir *Celebrate Survival*, Lon navigates us through his experiences with childhood abuse, the Vietnam War, PTSD, and living with an incurable disease. But he also brings out the humor in situations and provides interesting insight into historical events. Did you know that during the Vietnam War, helicopters dropped candy canes on the troops in the jungle? That must have been an interesting sight.

In Lon's story, it's apparent that his strong faith in God and love from his supportive family has carried him through the healing from physical and emotional wounds. He tells his story with honesty in hopes of encouraging others. I, for one, have been challenged and uplifted by his writings.

In an age when American men and women are still fighting in various conflicts while others recover from controversial wars and as people worldwide face disasters, this book is timely. Lon has endured much in his life but has decided not to let a dark past affect future moments. Instead, he writes inspirational poems and makes his life mission to uplift others. Lon believes each experience, good and bad, prepared him to be a poet. He's learned to live in the moment, because with Alzheimer's disease, you must.

Life is a journey filled with joy and sadness, success and failure. Perhaps my favorite sentence in this book is, "Life isn't always going to be a great success, but many small victories can be just as rewarding."

So here's to enjoying each moment of life and its many small victories. Thanks, Lon, for teaching me how to celebrate survival.

Cheers,
Rachel Turner
Communications Manager
Alzheimer's Association Washington State Chapter
Seattle, Washington

Introduction

My whole life is about survival .When you learn to celebrate survival, that's when you take it up a notch. I had to learn a lot about life to be able to understand how to celebrate survival. I had to learn to overcome the pitfalls of abuse as a child and a youth; and over my lifetime, with a lot of help from the Lord and many others, I was successful. Then came the divorces with my mom and dad. I learned the hard way as a young teenager how to raise a family of five siblings while my father was working two to three jobs.

As a young man of eighteen years old who loved his country with a passion, I joined the US Navy, which I thought would be a great adventure on the open seas. One of the only ships I was on was the hospital ship *USS Repose*. I was there because I got seriously wounded in jungles of Vietnam while serving as a corpsman with the marines.

From that time forward, I have been on a long ride of near-death experiences, also suicidal thoughts and attempts, severe PTSD (post traumatic stress disorder), several serious heart conditions, two brain surgeries, two brain aneurysm, agent orange, and now Parkinson's, Alzheimer's, and Lewy body dementia. I could find my self in a dark place, but I chose not to go there.

Surviving in Vietnam as a navy combat corpsman has helped me to understand the true value of life and how to use it to help others. It was an experience that many times I wish I could forget, but it still stays with me.

I believe that life is a gift from God, and we should live it to it's fullest.

I have been very blessed in my life with a wonderful family. My wife is my very best friend. I love her with all of my heart. She takes such great care of me, and I owe her so much. My son is one of the noblest men I have ever met and is a true gift in my life. My daughter has a zest for life. She has so much talent it's hard to imagine. I love her deeply. Our children have brought to us the purest grandchildren that any grandparent could ever possess. They are truly our greatest treasure. I know that God lives, and that Jesus is the Christ, and he has saved us all.

My life, I guess has helped prepare me to become a poet, and I sincerely hope you enjoy the poems I added to my short story of my life. My poems are written to inspire and uplift you and strengthen your faith. I pray that they do.

My journey in life will be much shorter than others, and my history may have had some dark moments, but I won't let it slow me down or define who I am.

I have learned something interesting that you will notice as you read my story. The further I go back in my life, the more I seem to remember. I think it is one of the few blessings I have with living with dementia.

I hope you will join me on my journey of my life and enjoy the many stories I have to tell. I pray you will learn something about yourself as I have learned about myself. One thing for sure I know, and that is I am "alive and thankful." I hope and pray you're the same.

Lon Cole
Author

1
Early Childhood

I was born August 23, 1948, in San Mateo, California. I am a true baby boomer. My dad was proud to have a son until he saw what I looked like. He said I was the ugliest baby he had ever seen. I spent my first year doing what every baby does everywhere, and that is cry, poop, eat, and cry again.

As the years passed on, my mom and dad became a regular baby factory. They averaged about a baby every other year until there were six of us, five boys and one little girl. After she was born, my dad got himself fixed.

During the big war, my dad was an electrician's mate on a flat-top aircraft carrier. He could see from his ship to the *USS Missouri*, the Japanese surrendering to General MacArthur. My dad's biggest claim to fame is that his carrier survived one of the worst typhoons of the US Naval Fleet. He saw smaller ships go down in the gigantic waves and never come back up. When he got out of his first hitch during World War II, he signed up for another during the Korean War as a submariner, which meant he was always away from home.

I had a good early childhood. My mother took very good care of us. I especially remember my aunt Martha. She was our baby sitter when my parents were gone. She was beautiful. She looked like Marilyn Monroe, and I had a big crush on her. One night, I learned her feelings about mice, when one of my brothers said there is a mouse in the kitchen. Before I knew it, my aunt Martha had all of us kids on top of the back of the couch, and she was holding a loaded .22-caliber rifle. In fact, her fear of mice was so unbelievable that she almost shot my dad when he came through the front door. She was so scared she wouldn't let go of the rifle and stayed on the back of the couch, and my mom joined her. My mother feared mice more than Aunt Martha. They stayed up on the couch until my dad caught the mouse and disposed of it.

During the Korean War, my dad's reserve unit was activated many times. He would be out on sea missions, and we would be home alone with Mom.

I had a close friend named George who was a few years older than me. He was a strange one. We would set up our army men in his garage and shoot at them with his pellet gun. He really chewed up the inside of his garage door, and I got hit several times from the ricochet pellets, and they really did hurt despite the heavy jacket I would wear. It stopped when I started using a garbage can lid to bounce them back at him.

After the Korean War, my dad worked several jobs, which meant a lot of moving.

It took awhile for my dad to find the right job. If you love your job, then you will work better, harder, and, in his case, longer hours. A wise man taught me to always show up to work a little early and leave a little late.

We settled down into a tract home in Palo Alto, California, All six of us kids gave Mom a run for her money, but she was a pretty tough lady. One day, I was playing army with some friends. One of my friends had a little brother who wanted to play with us. We told him to get lost. He didn't have a gun anyway. Well, he came back with a broken Coke bottle and said it was his bayonet. I told him to take off. That's when he decided to stab me with the Coke bottle and said, "I got you count to twenty." He really got me all right. I just ran into the house screaming and bleeding everywhere. My mother got one look at the blood and passed out cold. My neighbor had to bandage me up. I had to go to the doctor and get some stitches. He said that the stabbing just missed puncturing my lung, and at my age, that could have been fatal. That put a nix on playing war for a while.

My dad loved his job as a store manager of one the first supermarkets. It was located in Northern California. They seemed to have everything you needed besides tons of food items. I guessed they believed in one-stop shopping, even back in the fifties. One night, my dad brought me to work with him. He would let me stamp the prices on some of the canned goods he sold at the store. I remember that night well; it was Christmastime. That night, the store owner came up to me and said, "Lonnie, tonight you can have anything you want in the store." At first, I thought he was joking, but he was serious. We started with two shopping carts, and I started to fill them with everything an eight year old kid would dream of. That was until my dad came by and said, "Get meat." I think I got his hint. I filled up two carts; then we went back and got two more carts. When they were all full, I was getting tired, so we quit. It was a lot of fun, and the owner said, "Lonnie, that was so much fun." We had so much stuff and food that my dad didn't have room in his car to fit it all. Then the store owner gave my dad some cars keys and said, "There is a car in the back that is yours. Merry Christmas, Al." After that night, we became a two-car family.

One of my biggest adventures as a young kid in the fifties was when my dad took me to Disney 'and about one or two years after it first opened. It was just the two of us. We had a blast, and I got real close to my dad. Disney land and is a kid's dream come true. I also got to stay in some cheap, sleazy hotel rooms and eat lots of pancakes, hamburgers, and shakes. What an adventure that was.

My mom loved to go camping during the summer. All of us kids loved it too. She was a natural in the outdoors, and the park rangers were always asking her questions that they didn't know. She had all the right camping gear and brought lots of food, we kids loved to eat, and we loved the outdoors and the forest especially. When we weren't camping, we were at the community swimming pool. That's where I learned to swim. I was thrown into the deep water, and I had to swim back, or drown. After several tosses into the deep, I learned to swim pretty good. We repeated the same procedure for the rest of the Cole kids, including my sister Mary. She was the slowest to learn. We became really good swimmers. We really enjoyed our early years of summers.

My mom loved Christmas. She would get all excited and went all out on decorating the tree and the whole house. We always got good gifts. We would try anything to find out early what our presents were before Christmas morning. It was like our quest to find out. One night, my brother Billy camped out behind the overstuffed chair that my mom would sit on while watching TV. It was a perfect plan. He would stay there until they pulled out the gifts; then he would crawl back and give us the word on what we got. The plan failed because Billy fell asleep back there and didn't even get a peek. Finally, after many failed attempts to sneak a peek, my mother started putting a cot across the hallway on

Christmas ve where she slept for the night She was a light sleeper, and we were never able to get a sneak past her. The irony was that my mom always had to find out what her gifts were before Christmas.

My brothers had a dark side to them in their early years. My brother Ronnie was fascinated with fire and was always lighting something on fire. He even lit himself on fire. Once he almost burned up the whole garage. On one Christmas eve, he put a lit candle under my bed, and my bed caught on fire. I yelled out, "Mom, my bed is on fire." My mom just stayed in her cot, blocking the hallway, and told me to stay in bed and don't try any funny stuff. So I did. I guess the smoke from the fire woke her up. She ran into the bedroom and grabbed me out of the bed, then came back and put out the fire. Ronnie got quite the spanking for that caper, and fire days were over for him. Ronnie grew to be called Ron and, in his later years, became quite a wrestler. The truth is in the master's division of Greko-Roman wrestling. He won at least five national titles and became the world champion and traveled all over the world as a wrestler. Mike, on the other hand, had a different problem. He liked to hurt little animals when he was young. He was always flushing our turtles and fish down the toilet. One day, the parakeet got out of its cage, and Mom made us all look for the bird .Well, the parakeet landed on the dinning room table, and my brother Mike let out a scream. "I got it," he said. He was holding a fork in his hand and stabbed the little bird with it. He got a spanking, and we buried the bird. Mike grew out of that behavior. As he got older, he became one of the hardest workers I have ever met. He was very talented with his hands. He eventually became an owner of his own construction company. Unfortunately, he passed away in his late forties. I miss him so. My brother Billy was little, but he loved to fight. He would take on anyone that got in his way.

If they were bigger and older, he didn't care. Billy is still that way. He made an excellent marine. In fact, when he made it out of Marine Corps boot camp, his drill instructor told him he could beat the tar out of three sailors with one arm behind his back. So he went into a bar and followed what his drill instructor told him. He picked the three toughest sailors he could round up, and they beat him up bad and broke his nose. It didn't slow him down; he would always look for a good fight. He is still one tough marine (once a marine always a marine).

My brother Larry, when he was a baby, got his left arm caught in an old roller washing machine. He almost bled to death. It did cause brain damage, and he became mentally handicapped from that time on. Larry was the second oldest of the Cole kids. Larry would eat whatever was put on his plate. The rule was you can't leave the table until your plate was empty. Many nights, Larry would sit there eating his and all of our stuff we didn't like. All the food, mainly vegetables, would pile high. He would eat it all no matter how long it took. He still loves to eat but never gains weight. He is going strong and lives on his own. My little sister Mary was as cute as they can get. She was spoiled as a young girl, but now is the mother of four, and though she lives with a weak heart, it is a heart of gold.

Some days we would have carnivals in our backyard. We would charge two cents. Ronnie would start fires. My brother Mike would do n animal freak shows with our pets. Billy played the strongman. Larry would get dressed up in grown up clothes and chase everyone around like a crazy man. Mary would sing songs, especially "Kumbaya."I took in the money and was the master of ceremonies. Whoever came got their two cents' worth. I made sure of that. In the fifties, that was big money to a kid. It was going well until Ronnie set the garage on fire, though he got a standing ovation. He also tried to sell tickets for a nickel. That drove us out of business.

My mom ruled with an iron fist when we were bad, which was practically every day of our childhood. One afternoon, I told my mom that I was going to run away. My friends said, "don't worry. You can run away, then come back that night, and your parents would be all nice to you."So off I started running. I heard her yelling, "Get back here right now." That was when I turned on the speed. I had a great head start on her,except she climbed into the car and caught up with me. I got cornered in a dirt field, and she had me trapped. She got out of the car and yelled for me to get in the car. I was defiant and said, "No way." She then commenced to pick up dirt clods and started throwing them at me. It didn't take long before she zeroed in on me, and I was getting plastered with dirt clods despite my excellent dodging skills. I finally had enough, and I got into the car. She drove me home and gave me a licking, and I spent the night in the garage. I never tried to run away again. Nor did any of my brothers or sister try.

I had sort of a friend who was more like a bully than a friend. He would push me around a lot. Once, I told my mother, and she said, "Next time he does that, let him have it. His name was Bobby. We would play cowboys, and Indians out in the dirt mounds. He was always the cowboy, and I was the Indian who got killed. One afternoon, he was pushing me around on a dirt mound, and I had decided that I had enough, so I picked up a giant dirt clod and broke it over his head. He instantly went down and rolled down the dirt mound. He just lay there for a while, and I thought I had killed him. Then he stood up and started wailing at me. I thought he was a ghost. He was covered in the gray dirt. Then he started to chase me down the street. I dashed for home. boy, was I scared.

I made it to my front door, yelling, "Mom, help me. Bobby's going to kill me. She opened the screen door and let me in.

"You look like you've seen a ghost," she said. Bobby was right behind me. Mom slammed the screen door on him, which knocked Bobby on his butt. He went screaming all the way to his house, where his mom was waiting for him, and he got a bad spanking.

During Easter time, we were so excited about the Easter Bunny coming to our house on Easter eve. My brother Ronnie and I decided to stay up late and wait for him. Mom was over at our neighbor's house, our dad was at work, and everyone else was in bed. So Ronnie and I stayed up watching scary movies. It was about midnight when we heard a scratching at our front door. It didn't go away. It got louder. We were scared, but I opened the door to see what it was. There before my eyes was a live two foot rabbit just sitting there, staring at me. We ran to our rooms yelling, "The Easter Bunny is for real." When I told my mom the story, she just said, "You never know." I was real glad that we got our Easter baskets that year.

In our house, punishment was issued usually in group style from our dad, that is. When one got in trouble, all the boys got a spanking, but Mary was spared. It went by seniority which means I always got it first.

My dad would use his hand to spank us back then. The secret was to scream "bloody murder," while you were getting spanked. Mike, the youngest, would usually get off the easiest because by then dad's hand was pretty sore. One time, my brother Mike said, "I'm not going to cry no matter how hard you hit me." This got my dad really mad, and he was letting Mike really have it. Still he didn't cry, which got my dad really angry. No matter how hard he hit Mike, he just wouldn't cry. Well, my dad's hand was so sore he quit hitting Mike and told us to go to our rooms. We went to Mike's room to tell him how brave he was. Then Mike started pulling out magazines from the inside of the back of his pants. We just said, "Wow."

Then dad opened the door and caught Mike with the evidence, and he turned dark red with anger. Mike figured he was going to die, so he just looked at my dad with a smile. Then dad started laughing and closed the door. After that, my dad started using a belt.

As said before, Christmas was the best times at the Cole house. When I turned twelve I figured it was time for me to have rifle, a real . 22-caliber rifle. That's what I wanted for Christmas, along with a real sleeping bag, instead of the old bedroll made from blankets. Well, I caught my dad hiding what I wanted in the outside cabinet outside the house. He told me he was keeping it for our next-door neighbor's son who also was twelve years old. He was so lucky. I was heart broken. Christmas came, and everyone got what they wanted. All I got was a bunch of clothes. I was so disappointed. Then my dad said,Lonnie, I thought I saw some more gifts under the dinning room table. Go check it out. I made a beeline for the table, and sure enough, there were three gifts under the table. They all had my name on them. I opened them quickly; and to my surprise, I got a .22-caliber single shot rifle, a rifle cleaning set, and a real sleeping bag. It's been fifty-five years since that Christmas day, and I still have that rifle.

I wasn't much of a fighter when I was young. I could usually talk my self out of a fight. One day, I discovered a little Mexican fourth grader playing in our sixth grade playground. He was at least a head shorter than me and very quiet. So I decided to push him around some and told him to get out of our playground. Before I knew it, he turned around and faced me head on He let me have three to four punches in the face. *I* went down fast, *a*nd when I stood up, I had the start of a black eye, a bloody nose, and a chipped tooth. Nobody ever bothered him again, especially me. That was my last fight.

2
Later Childhood

My dad continued to change jobs a lot. We moved around a lot. Then finally we settled down in San Jose, California. Things were looking bright. Then one afternoon, our lives changed for the worst. The doorbell rang, and I opened the front door, and there she was. She must have been six feet tall, with long black hair. When I first saw her, I thought she was a bonafide witch. She gave me an awful and scary stare and asked, "Where are your parents ?"

I wanted to slam the door in her face, but instead I just called for Mom. Mom said hi, and she told Mom her name, and that she had just moved in next door. My mom showed her around the house. I knew something was now evil in our house, but I was helpless.

Life in San Jose went on. I got to know several of the neighbors, especially the girl who lived in the house that was behind our backyard. Yes, in the sixties, we liked girls my age. One of the days, I was talking to her across our fences. I heard fire trucks coming with their sirens blasting. I didn't think much about it, and I kept talking to this girl. Then the fire trucks parked in front of my house, and the firemen were coming out with hoses and axes. They went into our back door and came out with a burnt up pot that looked like it had been in a fire. Inside the pot was a large piece of charcoal that was supposed to be our dinner. I knew I was a dead duck because I was the one who put the frozen pot roast in the pot and turned up the heat. I ran toward the kitchen, but the fireman stopped me from going in. The fireman said, "You're very lucky that someone had enough common sense to smother out the fire with another pot." Then he said, "By the way, what kinda mother would let something like this happen?"

I thought, *the kind of mother who is going to kill her oldest son*, but I just said, "Mom isn't home." The fireman said he is going to leave her what turned out to be a very nasty note. There was no real fire damage, so the fireman left, and I went inside. I discovered after that my brother Larry smelt smoke in the kitchen. He went in and found the pot roast on fire. He turned off the heat, and quickly he got another pot and threw it over the pot on fire, which smothered the fire. Then Ronnie came into the kitchen, got scared, and called the fire department That didn't solve my problems, though. When Mom got home, she noticed the smoke damage in the kitchen and came out reading the nasty note left by the fireman. Then she said, "What the hell happened here?" My mother had a way with words. At that moment, I told one of my biggest lies ever. I told Mom that I was so sorry but that I did what she told me to do, and that was to put the frozen pot roast in the pot and warm it up. Before I knew it, it had caught on fire, so I was so scared that I put out the fire out by smothering it with another pot. I was so convincing that she believed me. She only yelled at me a lot and told me that I was brave and smart to smother the fire. I had to get to my brothers and swear them to secrecy. Larry forgot about the whole thing, but Ronnie, I had to buy his silence.

Well, time moved on, and I needed some money. What kid doesn't? I started a business babysitting. I got a job sitting for my neighbors on New Year's Eve. I got paid extra because they wouldn't be home till 1:30 a.m. At about 10:30 p.m., I heard a big crash from the back-sliding door. The kids were already in bed, so I went to check out the noise. To my shock, there was a Mexican man on the other side of the glass door. He was in a panic, and all he had on was his underwear. He was banging on the door and begging me to let him in. I got scared and called the police. They came very quickly, handcuffed the man, and took him away. They said he was drunker than a skunk. I found out later that the man had got into a serious fight with his wife, and she chased him out of his house with a huge kitchen knife. It got real quiet after that. There was no TV, but at midnight, it got real noisy with noisemakers, fireworks, and people screaming, "Happy New Year." I had nothing to make noise with. All I had was this pot of instant mashed potatoes I had made. I went outside, screaminn

Happy New Year, and splattered three or four garages with mashed potatoes. I never got caught for that one.

At eleven years old, I became a boy scout. Boy I was excited. I remember my first hike. My mom fixed me up with all the gear I needed, courtesy of the army surplus. I had my old knapsack with my lunch and snacks in it and a real army canteen. I was ready for anything. It was a fiv mile hike, two and a halfmiles out and two and a halfmiles back. I made it to almost the turn around point, and I couldn't go any farther no matter what I did. My legs were like rubber. I was all out of food, and I had a little bit of water. I just sat down against a tree. I figured it was where I was going to die. Scouts would walk by me, going both ways. I just told them, "This is where I'm going to die." They just started laughing and kept going by. I didn't think it was funny. Then for a while, it got really quiet. There was no one walking by. I got really scared I figured I would die there and a mountain lion or bear would eat me up. Then I heard someone coming down the trail, and he was whistling. He stopped right in front of me and asked, "What's going on?"I recited my same response that "I can't go any farther, so I guess I am going to die here."

"We can't have that happen. You got any water?"

"Yes, a little." I said

"Can we share it?" He asked

Of course." I said

"Then climb on." He said

What do you mean?" I asked

He told me to climb on his back and he will carry me. So I did, and down the trail we went, liittle Lonnie on the back of Big Cooper. We would walk for a while, then stop and rest, then continue to walk. Toward the end of the trail, we stopped .Cooper said, "Cole, let's walk the rest of the way together." I knew he wanted no one to know that he had carried me. I remember at the end everyone was cheering. I never saw Cooper again, but I'll never forget him.

After my first hike, I had my first camp out overnight. I again came well equipped with my army surplus pack, bedroll, little pup tent, a flashlight, canteen, and my foil wrapped hamburger dinner. I set up my tent and my bedroll (couldn't afford a sleeping bag). Then I started to build a fire. All the other scouts had canned food, and the scoutmaster had a Coleman stove to heat up their food. I didn't care. I thought as soon as I get the fire going, I will have my dinner, and, boy, was I hungry. Then it started to poor down rain. I had everything to build a big fire, but everything was wet, so the fire wouldn't start. I used up so many of my matches, and I was in a big mess. I tried and tried to start my fire while everyone else was eating their dinner. Then the assistant scoutmaster approached me.

He said, "What's the matter, Lonnie?"

I said, almost crying, "I can't get my fire started, and I can't cook my dinner, and I am getting really hungry."

Then he looked to see if anyone was watching us. He went to his car and pulled out a flare and lit it and stuck it into my fire until it was blazing. Then he quietly put out the flare and put it back into his trunk. I had the biggest fire in the campsite, and, boy, was my foil dinner starting to smell good. All the other scouts came over to my campfire and said, "Boy, whatever you're having, it sure smells good." After that, you might say I was a happy camper.

Life wasn't always rosy for me. My dad and mom started having problems and were fighting a lot. I spent a few months alone with my aunt and uncle. It was not a pleasant experience. They drank a lot. Years passed by, and we decided to move into Grandma Cole's house in Burlingame, California. Sadly, though, my mom insisted that her best friend Molenda and her two kids had to come along. Molenda had gotten a divorce from her crazy husband, who really believed his house was haunted. He even had ghost chasers come to his house. We watched the whole thing. It was scary to say the least. Then my dad put his foot down and told my mom that either Molenda and her bratty kids go, or he goes. Shortly after that, they got a divorce. It was a sad time for us all. My dad was gone.

Mom, Molenda, and all the kids moved into Grandma Cole's house. We saw our dad on the weekends. Rich, Molenda's son, became the meanest guy I ever would know. He would abuse and torture us Cole kids all the time. One of the things Rich like to do after we got spanked was he would make us stand in a corner of the house for hours without any meals or water. One weekend, my dad came early and caught Rich abusing my brother Ronnie. My dad ran across the yard, picked up Rich with both hands, and threw him across the yard to the sidewalk. Then he went up to him, grabbed him by the neck, and told him if he ever lays a hand on any of his kids again that he would kill him. We were proud of our dad that day. Rich must have believed my dad, because the beating and abusing stopped. Shortly after that, my dad moved in, and my mom and Molenda and her kids moved out with Mary. I loved my mom and missed her. I guess even moms are human and make mistakes. I knew she loved us, and in her heart she was a kind woman. We all loved her so. Now it's dad and the Cole boys. I became the mom of the house. My dad still worked two jobs. I would run the house on the weekdays, and he would run the house on the weekends. I would prepare the meals and supervise the chores, which got expensive for me. I had to pay my brothers to do the work. I made sure my brothers got to bed on time. My sister joined us a year later.

3
High School Years

I took care of my brothers and sister for almost all of my high school years. It was a lot of chores every day. I was pretty active in sports and in my church. My night off was Friday night, and every Friday night, I would go to Borden's to buy a large bag of french fries, then walk back and go to the recreation teen dance at the recreation hall at least until I was old enough to go to the church dances.

One day, I convinced my mom to drive me across the bay to the Oakland Temple. It was over a two hour drive. I wanted to attend a youth church fireside. She said yes, but I had to get my own way back. She did her part and left me at the temple site. Everything appeared to be closed, and I was worried that I had the wrong day and that I had no way to get home. Cell phones didn't exist back then. I was walking through the temple grounds thinking that I was about ninety plus miles from home, and I am all alone. I started to pray that something would happen to help me. As I continued walking, I heard the faint sound of music coming from the end of the hallway. I opened the door, and inside were hundreds of youth and adults singing "The Spirit of God Like a Fire Is Burning." I found an empty seat and joined in with the singing. I was no longer alone and lost. The Lord heard my prayers and answered them.

The next year, in 1963, I was chosen from my church to dance in a national dance festival at University of Utah. They could only take four couples, and I got chosen. It was a big deal, and we had to drive all the way to Salt Lake City, Utah, and I got to spend a couple of nights there. There were about eight thousand kids at this dance festival. We practiced for two days, and that's when I got introduced to Colonel Sanders Kentucky fried chicken. Boy, it was "finger lickin' good." I still love that chicken. On the morning of the performance, it was raining cats and dogs. Our dance leader had us offer a prayer to our heavenly Father to stop the rain from falling during the performance. Then suddenly the rain stopped, and the clouds parted, and the sky was clear. The sun came out and dried everything that was wet. In fact, the sun was so bright I got a bit of sunburn Before the finale, I lost my partner, and I was in a panic trying to find her. Then I saw her from behind, so I jumped and picked her up in the air, and when I turned her around, she was someone else. She socked me good, and I went down. "I'm sorry," I said. Then my partner found me, and we finished the finale to a standing ovation. It was awesome. Then the clouds came back while we were leaving the field, and so did the hard rain. It was a small miracle that I won't forget.

I loved playing football for my school. In one of the games, my girlfriend Jennifer came to watch me play. I didn't play much the first half, but in the second half, I was playing linebacker. In one of the plays, they faked out our whole team except me. Then they formed a huge V formation. They headed right for me. I hit them dead center, and they went down, and so did I. When all the players piled off me, I must have been knocked out cold, because when I woke up I was on the sideline on one knee with a bottle of smelling salts. We lost the game, but my girlfriend told me she felt so sorry for the poor boy who got knocked out and was carried off the field. I told her that was me. She said, "Why do you play such a dangerous game anyway?" Jennifer was my first love, and I worshiped her. My new step mom, Pat, decided that Jennifer and I had to break up. That really hurt. She was my best friend. It's no fun losing your best friend. My dad had married Pat about three years after he divorced my mom. Their marriage didn't last long. She had two boys of her own, whom she always favored over the Cole kids.

I was going to seminary in the morning, which was a religious class we took in high school and sponsored by the church. One morning, I got my wake up times mixed up, and I stepped out the front door two hours early. It was very cold, but I didn't want to wake up Pat because she would get really mad and ground me for a month. I just waited for my ride and almost froze to death.

I decided to take German in high school because I had the hots for one of the girls in the class. I did very poorly in class, but Dr. Getzol, our teacher, liked me, so she gave me a C minus for my grade so that I would take the next semester of German. Instead, my girlfriend quit German and went into choir, so guess what I did? I dropped out of German and joined the choir. Dr. Getzol was furious. I learned to love the choir.

My step mother, Pat, ended my sports career because I got one D plus in typing. I was heart broken. I loved football and wrestling, but it was no more. So I signed up for drama.

There were lots of girls in drama, and I was pretty good at it. I was told by my drama teacher that I had a powerful voice. I starred in a couple of school plays. I had dreams of being a famous movie star.

Drama and choir helped me get though my Junior year. During my senior year, y dad and Pat got divorced. I was back as the weekday mom of the house. Then my dad moved me out of my school to a new city, so I didn't get to graduate with all my friends, and I was devastated. I started going to Awalt High School. While I was at Awalt High School, I joined the US Navy Reserve. It was my mother's idea. I went to a two week boot camp during my Christmas break, and I went to a two week cruise for my spring break. I also went out for track. I did the shot put and discus.

I did pretty good with the shot put. One time, I was carrying the shot put between my legs and acting like the man to impress two girls walking by. Some jerk had to go and throw a shot put right at me. I must have jumped ten feet up to avoid being hit by the oncoming shot put. At the same time, I jammed the shot put into my groin. I almost became a soprano instead of a bass for choir. The girls just started screaming, "Are you okay?" I did my best to just smile back at them. Needless to say, I was hurting for weeks, and for a while, I walked very slowly. I must admit that my real claim to fame was with the discus. I was the only one ever to kill a gofer in midflight with my discus. My coach said that I should be in the new *Guinness Book of Records*. It was kind of cool. The girls thought it was gross.

The day I graduated from high school, I wasn't sure that I was even going to graduate. I opened my envelope to see if I made it. I let out a yelp when I realized I had graduated. That didn't go over well with the principal. I enjoyed my high school years, but I was really busy taking care of my family. I have the greatest respect for mothers and all the hard work they do.

4
The Navy Years

While I was in high school, I had been in the naval reserves for over a year. At my boot camp, we were called two week wonders. I was chosen to be the master at arms for our unit. That meant that I was responsible for keeping our barracks clean. If I failed, I was dead meat. We would have fire drills every day at certain times. When the alarm went off, we were to drop everything and get in formation outside the barracks. Our drill instructor made sure we moved fast. Any goof ups and we would be doing pushups till our arms would fall off. Well, one day during personal clean up, I hit the wrong switch, and I activated the fire alarm. Everybody exited the barracks like lightning and got in formation. Most were naked with a towel wrapped around them. Some still had shaving cream on their faces, and everyone was furious. I heard some guys say they were going to kill the sucker that set off that alarm. I didn't want to get murdered, so I joined in on the complaining like I had no idea who had done it. If anyone had found out it was me, I would have gotten a shower party at least which is when a bunch of recruit sailors grab you while in the shower and scrub you down with floor scrubbing brushes..I think it is as bad as being tarred and feathered and is very painful and humiliating.

Then there was my two-week cruise on a old World War Two destroyer. I enjoyed every minute of it, especially when I would sit outside in my underwear by a hot air vent and watch the waves. Everyone else would walk by freezing, and they thought I was the crazy one. Half of the crew got seasick and was always barfing over the side. This went on for most of the cruise. I ate and slept just fine and never got sick. One day, I and another hospitalmen were standing at the bow of the ship. We looked up to the bridge and saw our captain laughing his head off. When we turned back around, we got sideswiped by a wave of seawater, and it knocked us on our butts and almost washed us off the ship. We didn't think it was so funny.

I still loved the cruise. We had to bury at sea a young marine who was killed in Vietnam. We were all on deck in our dress whites. When they went to spread the ashes onto the ocean, the wind flared up and blew his ashes all over everyone, including the skipper and the family attending the service. It was awful, even the seagulls went after the ashes. That was not a good experience.

When I graduated from high school, I got my orders right away for two years of active duty. I was to report to San Diego Naval Hospital for four months of hospital corpsman training. It was hard work for a young eighteen-years old, but we had a great motivator to finish the course. That was if we failed we were sent to riverboat duty in Vietnam. The life expectancy of a riverboat sailor was about five minutes, I was told. The training was really tough. I had to work hard to make it. I am glad that I stuck to it. We learned a lot about medicine and how to treat people who had all types of pain, injuries and sickness.

Once I finished my schooling, I was assigned orders for San Diego Naval Hospital. I was first assigned to a ward of thirty patients. Most of them were old senile (now called Alzheimer's) guys who had retired from the navy or the marines. They would do the strangest things. One retired chief petty officer was checking out of the ward, and, boy, was his suitcases heavy. It was as if he had filled them up with rocks.

I asked him, "What do you have inside here?"

He said, "Newspapers."

I asked him why. He told me that he's going to soak the newspapers in hot water until all the ink comes off. Then he will inject the stuff into raw eggs, and when you fry the eggs, you can read the eggs like a newspaper. Most of the men came into our ward lean and mean. When they left, they were skin and bones, and many went to the morgue.

One very large and strong and young sailor on our ward suffered from grand mal seizures. I was escorting him to the movie house to watch a movie. On the way, he had a full-blown seizure and went down fast and was shaking all over. He started to choke on his tongue, so I put a padded tongue blade to depress his tongue down. He quickly snapped the tongue blade in two. Then I decided to use my thumb to open his mouth so he could breathe. That was a big mistake. He tried to bite off my thumb. He came close, and I still have the scar to prove it. It took five sailors to hold him down so he wouldn't hurt himself. Then the seizure stopped, and he stood up with all five of us holding on to him. We were in worse shape than he was.

I then got transferred to the emergency room, which was always busy, being it claimed to be the largest ER in the country. I worked all three shifts. One night, while I was working the front triage desk, two men came in and stood at the front of my desk.

"How can I help you?" I asked.

The younger man said to me, "My father tried to kill himself."

I kindly asked him, "What kind of pills did he take?"

The son said, "He didn't take pills. He shot himself in the head." I looked at the old man. He looked perfectly normal. I told the old man not to joke around like this. Then the old- timer opened his mouth, and a pool of blood poured out onto my desk. It turned out that he had sucked on the barrel of a .38-caliber pistol and pulled the trigger. It missed his brain and exited out the soft tissue of the back of his neck He was a walking miracle. He spent a few days in the hospital and was discharged from hospital in fairly good health, and of course, he had a referral for a psychiatrist. The emergency room was always crazy, and hard to believe.

Another night, while at the front desk, a wife of a sailor came into the ER. She was accompanied by three US Marines, and they were all drunk. She reported to have horrible menstrual cramps. While she was waiting for the doctor, she decided to do a striptease act with the three marines singing for the music part of her show. All the staff who was free came out to watch the show. There was quite a crowed out there.

A lot of the simple things done by doctors and nurses now were done by a corpsman then, I had to sew up cuts and gashes, administering medicines, drawing blood, and many more medical procedures.

One late night, my drill instructor from combat medic school came with his arm all cut up. It looked like someone had broken a bottle over his arm about a week or so, before he came in, there was still glass embedded in his arm, and it look like it was infected. My job was to cut out all the bad, infected skin and glass, then clean and sew up the cuts and clean up the blood, mess, and bandage him. I got nervous just standing by him. He was one tough drill sergant He was Force Recon and had been to Vietnam three times. I started to inject some painkiller into his cuts. Then he said, "No needles, Doc. I can take it. Don't worry." So I started working on him, and he just sat there all quiet. He showed no pain at all. I was a nervous wreck. When I was done, it took over and hour to do. He stood up said, "Thanks, Doc. Good luck in Vietnam" and walked out the door. He didn't even break a sweat.

We had several druggies come into the ER, and they could be quite entertaining. We had one swinging a sword, one who shot himself in the leg in the ER, and one who was sure he was God. Another thought he was Billy Joel the singer. We also had the usual cardiac and brain injuries and, of course, gunshot and stab wounds. Some nights, it seemed like a war zone. Some of our patients died, but many were transferred to the wards so they could die there. We did save most of our patients.

Later that year, the hospital started to have a serious drug problem amongst the corpsmen and staff. A major drug ring appeared to come from the hospital staff and corpsmen themselves. I was recruited and asked to be an undercover narc for the hospital. I was casual friends with one of the corpsmen who was suspected to be the large drug dealer. No one could catch him, though. No one ever suspected me because I was the only corpsman who admitted being a virgin and appeared to be very naiveand all innocent

During my time off I would go surfing with one of corpsmen buddies who was Hawaiian. I almost drowned once when my surfboard popped up out of the wave and split my head open. I tried to go back out into the waves, but I was bleeding so bad that people came and pulled me out of the water and helped me back to the beach. Later I had to get some stitches above my right eye. I wasn't a very good surfer, but I had a lot of fun.

While I still was stationed at the naval hospital, I got orders for field medic school. There, we were taught how to be combat medics for Vietnam. We knew sooner or later we would be called to go. We worked hard, and I paid attention throughout the course. We learned many ways to save marines' lives in combat. During the course, they would have us run very hard, so hard that one day I started barfing up all over myself and the other men. When we made it to chow line, I was starving .The word got out that we were going to have steak. I had only had steak once in my life, so I was excited. I got to the serving line, and it turned out to be liver and onions (I despise liver).

I said, " No, thank you."

My drill sergeant said face to face, "Sailor, you will eat those liver and onions, and they will taste good."

I said, "Yes, sir."

I took one bite and started puking up the liver. Several of my fellow corpsmen saw me puking, so they started to puke. I had to do hundreds of push ups that day. After combat medic school, I went back to the naval hospital, and I worked my butt off.

I went back to being an undercover narcotic agent for the CID. I got a lot of guys busted, but I couldn't get the main dealer who was stationed at the hospital as a corpsman. We knew he was smuggling needle and syringes to Mexico in trade for some serious drugs. It turned out that he and I went to corpsman school together. He liked me a lot, and I thought he never suspected me as a narc. Some of the other narcs were really getting hurt pretty bad. One even got stabbed, but she survived. One day, I was out on a big field, listening to Glen Campbell music. I was all alone on that field, which, at one side, had a steep drop off to it. I saw the drug dealer start to walk across the field toward me. I thought, this is it. *He's coming out here to take me out.* I tried to act cool when he got very close. Then he said, "We know who the narc is, Cole."

I tried to act surprised, and I said, "Who is he?"

He stared straight into my eyes and said, "The narc is you." I looked around and realized that this could be my last day on earth. I told him that he was right, and I got ready for the worst. Then he put his hand on my shoulder and said, "Cole, I really love you, guy. I don't want you to get hurt, but you got to get out of here very fast because they will be coming for you soon." Then he just turned around and left me standing there. I got to the CID guys as fast as I could. I told them what happened and that I got to get transferred out ASAP. The best they can do was two weeks. That wasn't good enough. I needed to get out in a couple of days at the best. They told me the only way to get out quick is to volunteer for Vietnam. I figured I had a better chance in Vietnam than I had staying at the hospital, so I agreed. I was out in three days, sweating every day I was there.

5
Vietnam

I got a thirty-day leave before being shipped to Vietnam. During that thirty-day leave, I had a lot to think about. *Was I really ready for this?* I spent most of my time at home practicing driving the family car. I took my driving test and passed the test by sher luck or maybe because I told the tester I was going to Vietnam and I wanted my driver license in case I didn't come back. I also almost got married to my girlfriend, which I'm glad I didn't, because she dumped me while I was in Vietnam.

Then I was off to Vietnam as a combat corpsman. My trip to Vietnam took only a few days. I spent three days in Okinawa for climate adjustment, and, boy, it was hot and humid. There wasn't much to do. I was happy to go, but I was really nervous. Then I flew out and landed in Da Nang, Vietnam, in October of 1968. Da Nang is in the northern part of South Vietnam. Within one day, I was given my combat gear, a medic bag, and a .45-caliber pistol. Then I was put on a helicopter heading for the DMZ. I remember the smell of the diesel fuel; and it was hot, humid, and full of jungle. I was assigned to Hotel Company second Platoon part of the Second Battalion Ninth Marines. Our job was to support an artillery base pointed toward the DMZ just above Khe Sanh I learned quickly that my marines loved their corpsman. That was because we took care of them when they were sick or wounded or worse. Still I had to be officially initiated into the platoon. My turn came after my second day. I was given a really nice bunker to sleep in. It was set up for only one person. So I set up shop and got ready for a good sleep. That night, I kept feeling dirt fall on me all over my legs, my belly, and my chest. Then I heard a hissing noise above my head. I got out my flashlight and looked up. There was the biggest rat I have ever seen. Then I could see dozens of rats all through the bunker. Boy, did I get out fast. Outside was what appeared to be the entire platoon minus the CO and gunnery sergeant. One of the squad leaders said, "Doc, you stayed in there longer than anyone before. After that, they treated me very well, and I took good care of them. In fact, I grew to love my marines like family.

Then came the allay patrols and all-night ambushes. It took two weeks to get used to all the hiking we did. I also had the runs for a month. I couldn't get my pants down in time to go. I did a lot of laundry that month, which was done by hand.

On the start of my third week, we got hit by a very precise mortar attack. It was a terrible pounding. Then I heard someone call out, "Corpsman." I went out to find the wounded marine while the mortar rounds were still falling. I wasn't very smart, I must admit, but it was my duty. I found two marines wounded. One marine look like he was a goner. The other marine was my roommate. His name was Private Butts. We had become good friends. I started plugging up wholes in both of the marines. Butts looked like he might make it. Then I heard and felt a horrible explosion right next to me about five or less feet away. Then everything went silent, and I couldn't hear anything. Everything was like in slow motion. My ears were ringing. I was somewhat confused, but I went back to Butts, trying to bandage his neck when I noticed a large whole in the top of his head. I could see his brains. Deep down inside, I knew he was gone, but I started CPR on him and the other marine. I got them to some stretchers and climbed on to make sure they were secure. Then suddenly the helicopter took off with me on it. I was along for the ride, and I was not a happy corpsman. I continued CPR on both the marines. It was so hard that at one time I had to swallow the bloody vomit to keep from choking. I just could give up trying to help them. When we landed at the battalion aid station, a doctor came out and quickly sent my marines to grave registration. "They're dead," he said. I was so depressed, and it hurt me so deeply. I had to work my way back to the platoon. It took hours to get back, and by the time I got back, the battle was over. I felt horrible to be away from my marines. My platoon commander, one the best leaders I have ever met, approached me. He told me that he had never seen until today a mortar round land so close to someone and all the shrapnel go in the opposite direction, and that I was one very lucky corpsman. Then he told me he had some bad news. He said he was going to write you up for the Bronze Star. But if he did that, he would have to report me for leaving the scene of the battle. I told him what happened and how bad I felt. He believed me. We decided to call it a wash no Bronze Star, no report.

Vietnam was a hellhole. We spent almost all of our time in the jungle. We would get a few days a month in one of the rear bases, like LZ Stud, to get real hot food, maybe a shower, and a little rest. Most of the days were long patrols and night ambushes. I learned a corpsman job is never done. The actual firefights were one part of Vietnam. The daily living with elephant grass, leaches, lots of very poisonous snakes and insects, the unbearable humid heat, heavy monsoon rains, of course the blood-sucking mosquitoes, and much more. I worked hard to keep my marines healthy along with trying to survive myself. I was told after four months I would be rotated out to a rear area. That is if I survived. To be truthful, it would be hard for me to leave those great men.

There were many times that I really was petrified in Vietnam. Once we were on a night ambush, and we all had to take our turns staying awake and watching for the enemy. When it was my turn, our gunny sergeant told me, "Don't fall asleep. The enemy can sneak up on you and cut your throat before you let out a sound." Then I sat there just thinking about what he said, and why Iwas in the middle of the jungle in the middle of the night just waiting to get my throat cut. It was pitch-black I couldn't see my hand in front of me. I was holding a M16 on fully automatic, waiting and trying to hear VC or NVA sneaking up on me. All I heard in the middle of the night was the many jungle sounds. I was so tired, but I had to stay awake for two hours. The rest were all asleep. I was so scared that if I would have had to pee, I would have peed my pants. When the gunny tapped my shoulder, I quickly turned around and almost blew his head off. He just calmly said, "Doc, lay the rifle down slowly." I was ready to get some sleep. I figured if the enemy got here at least I would die in my sleep.

Another time that I was really scared was again in the middle of the night. I was woken up from a very hard sleep. We were at our base camp. I was told to get in line with several marines because our LP (listening post) was in trouble. Again total blackness and dead silences. Somehow I got in the line, but I couldn't move. I was so scared that I just couldn't move my feet. My marines had to push me really hard to get me moving. Fear is a powerful emotion.

Sometimes I would go many a days and nights without sleep. One night, I finally got to get some well-earned sleep. Then one of my marines woke me up and said, "Get up, Doc. It's Holder. He's been shot." I was so tired I briefly argued with him about getting up. He pulled me to my feet, and I grabbed my medic bag, and I followed him running down a very steep hillside. At the bottom was Holder, lying. He was surrounded by some really worried marines. Holder was really all shot up. It was really dark and pouring down rain. I found myself plugging up, sucking chest wounds. It was a terrible and helpless feeling. I could hear the air leaking from his lungs. Corporal Morgan (Later awarded the Medal of Honor posthumous) kept yelling, "Don't let him die, Doc." I tried everything I could, but I couldn't save him, and he died. That hurt me so much. That morning I checked his body. He had about twinty holes in his body and chest. It turned out that Holder was accidentally shot by his good friend. Holder was snoring, and his friend leaned over on his M16 to wake him. It was an ambush that night. His friend had his M16 on fully automatic, and the trigger housing got caught on a bamboo branch, and he emptied the whole clip of M16 rounds into Holder.

There was nothing he could do. He couldn't stop it, and it happened so fast. That night, I had to treat Holder's friend for serious shock. I had to rock him like a little baby to soothe him. I told him, "Don't worry. Holder is up in heaven now." We eventually got him a medivac out, along with Holder. Holder was one of the nicest marines I ever met. His laugh was contagious. I will never forget him.

Another ambush I went on was in a kill zone. It was a night ambush. A kill zone means if anything moves, shoot first and ask questions later. It was set up as a crisscross ambush. So whoever came into our kill zone didn't have a chance. Then after about two hours of waiting, I heard all hell break loose. When the shooting stopped, there were two NVA soldiers lying on the trail. One was killed instantly. The other was wounded very bad. They asked me to do what I could to save him so they could interrogate him later. He was shot up pretty bad, and I didn't think he was going to make it. He was screaming at the top of his lungs. My squad leader said,Doc, shut him up. His sreaming will give away our position to the whole NVA army." I tried everything that I could to help him, but he wouldn't stop screaming. My marines kept yelling at me to shut him up. I finally lost my cool and yelled out, "I can't save him. Just shoot him." That's what they instantly did. They shot him several times in the head. His head just collapsed like a balloon popping. I got sick as I saw it happen. They took the two bodies and laid them in the open on the trail and continued the ambush, waiting for more to come like nothing had happened. All night, I had to just stare at two dead men, especially the one NVA whom I had the marines shoot. This experience has haunted me for over forty-five years. I was not the same after that.

One day, we got to go back to the rear area out of the jungle for a couple of days. Everyone was getting drunk. I didn't drink, but when my marines asked for some pain pills, which they were always doing. I don't know to this day why, but this time, I gave them out and took some myself. That was a big mistake. I got stoned, which for me was a new experience. I sat down by some marines who had a campfire going and were singing some songs, including, of course, the Marine Corps hymn. There was one marine who just sat there quietly. Then he stood up and walked into the clouds. Then the clouds turned into a pack of dogs that started chasing me all through the tents. I do remember yelling, "Somebody, help me." I woke up many of the marines, who while trying to sleep it off angrily said, "Shut up, Doc. Go get some sleep." The next thing I remember was waking up in the morning on the side of a road in a ditch full of diesel, water, and mud. I felt horrible. Never again did I listen to my marines about pain pills.

Crazy things happen in Vietnam. If you did something to someone, they found unique ways to get even. We had a supply sergeant who was crazy as they can get. Many times at night he would take his KA-Bar knife and a pistol and sneak out into the jungle to find the enemy while the rest of us slept. Nobody tried to stop him. Sometimes he would be so tired that he couldn't get his job done, and that affected us all. A few of us waited until he crawled out into the jungle. then we killed a giant centipede and put it into his hoochon top of his rubber mattress. They are usually two to three feet long and very poisonous. In the middle of the night, he crawled into his hooch. He discovered the centipede and shot it up with his .45-caliber pistol, which destroyed his rubber mattress and poncho liner. He decided not to leave his bed at night anymore. Another time we had a really dumb and crazy marine who almost scared us to death. We were playing cards, and some of the marines were smoking pot. I like it when they smoke pot, because I would win more of the card games. Anyway, we were playing cards in a real deep bunker, and this crazy marine looked down into the whole above the bunker and said, "I have a surprise for you, guys." He then threw a hand grenade right into the middle of our card game. We just sat there frozen. Nobody made a move even though the firing pin was gone from the hand grenade; we were all frozen. Several minutes seemed to pass before we realized the grenade was a dud. Luckily, he had taken out the explosives. We had to get this guy out of our unit ASAP. So while he was on a LP (listening post), some of the marines reversed a clamor mine and started making some noise in the bushes in front of him. He stood up and yelled, "Clamor," and then he pushed the button. It exploded, luckily with only a little bit of the shrapnel coming to him. He only sustained minor flesh wounds, but enough to get him medivaced out of the jungle. He never came back to our platoon.

I didn't approve of my fellow comrades' behavior, but I was sure glad to see him go.

One of my many patrols was a twelve man patrol, which meant they took a corpsman. We ended up in Cambodia, in a very thick jungle. We found a beautiful stream and pool of water by a huge rock. The patrol leader decided this is where we needed to stop for a while. This was not according to our orders, but he didn't care. Because we were in enemy territory, we posted a guard and gave him all are weapons to keep them dry and call in our checkpoints. The rest of us played in the water. We even played water polo with a giant grapefruit. After a while, our guard got mad and stood up on the huge rock and yelled, "What about me?" He then slipped off the rock and fell into the pool of water. At first we thought it was funny until we saw that he was drowning with all the weight of our weapons on top of him. He was madder than hell when we pulled him up. Then we all started laughing again. By the time we got back from our patrol, we were all dry and no one was the wiser.

One time I was on a full-platoon forced hike. That means a very long patrol. It felt like about fifty miles. In one day. It was very hot.

Over half the way, though, I just gave up and sat down by a rock. Does that sound familiar? I couldn't go any farther. I knew my marines felt the same, but a marine never quits. Well, this sailor did. I said, "This is as far as I go. I will catch up later."

My gunny sergeant said, "Doc, get up right now."

I told him I was not taking another step. Big mistake on my part. The old gunny pulled out his .45-caliber pistol and pointed it at my head. He said, "Iff you don't get up now, I will have to shoot you."

I said, "Go ahead. I don't give a damn." Well, I looked up at him, and I noticed he was starting to cry as he was getting ready to pull the trigger. I knew then he wasn't bluffing.

Well, I got up very quickly and was on my way. Every time I would start to slow down, the gunny would walk by and just pat on his . 45. That's all the motivation I needed to keep going.

I remember being on a huge patrol on the day they celebrated the Marine Corps birthday. We had two reporters from *Life* magazine with us. We were coming to the end of the patrol, and then the head fire team started shooting into the jungle. The whole platoon froze, and a battle started. Our squad leader called in artillery and air support, and when it was all over, no enemy was found. All we had was a dead wild boar. We had to carry that pig back with us. Orders from our company commander himself. I ended up humping three marines gear with my own so they could carry that pig. They decided they were going to cook that pig to celebrate the Marine Corps birthday. I think it was really to impress the reporters, because when they left our company, the commander said, "Get rid of the pig." We did have hot chow all that we wanted . And Santa dropped us candy canes from a helicopter.

I had been in country about four and a half months. I was the senior corpsman in the company. I was very proud of my marines. They were great in a firefight, and I feel they were the best our country had to offer. I loved serving with them.

Then we walked into some real mess. It was part of Operation Dewey Canyon—the last marine major offensive of the Vietnam War.

We were in severe enemy territory. I declined my rotation out and was reassigned to third platoon. I was the most experienced medic. I missed the second platoon, but they needed me elsewhere. While on a company patrol, we entered the A Shau Valley. That day, we came under a severe enemy ambush. Several casualties were sustained. I was quite busy that afternoon, patching up marines. The fight was intense, but I was in the zone. Then someone yelled out, "Charge!" The next thing I know I am running down the trail with a bunch of crazy Marines. Then the column came to a halt, and I heard more shooting, then the scream, "Corpsman!" again. It came from way up front, so I ran up to the point fire team. I found our point man for the whole company was out in the open and was gutshot. He was screaming, "Doc, help me." So I grabbed my medic bag and ran out to the wounded marine and started patching him up. The next thing I know I heard a small explosion, and I am flying in the air when I hit the ground I could smell the burnt flesh hanging in the branches of an old tree trunk. It was really stinging, especially my shoulder and upper back. I noticed I had a wound in my side, which I found out later I got when we first got ambushed. I also had a larger wound on my right shoulder. I could feel my shoulder joint was exposed. It really was hurting. I was bleeding pretty bad and started going into shock. Meanwhile, I still had a wounded marine to take care of. So I started working on him. Then I would start getting dizzy from the loss of blood. So I would have to lean against a little tree trunk with a makeshift bandage to slow down the bleeding, then back to my marine, and this went on for several minutes. I could see the tracer rounds over my head from both sides. Several of them were hitting the tree trunk and around our exposed bodies. It didn't look very good for both of us. Then the platoon commander crawled out and grabbed my wounded marine by his backpack strap and pulled him to safety. Now I was the only one left out there. I heard a scream, "Pull back," which I guess they did. I was on my own. I waited for them to come and get me, but I guess they were getting shot up so bad they couldn't come out to get me. I was crouching down behind the tree trunk while the shooting increased from the enemy's side. I called out but got no answer. I knew I had to get out of there, or I would be a goner or worse get captured. We knew what they did to enlisted men, even Boxis, so I decided I would make a run for it. Now I was in shock, so what I did next was a little crazy. I got up on my feet, closed my eyes, spun around a couple of times, and started running and screaming. In my mind, I figured I would get to the bushes I saw, or I would get shot dead. Either way, I was better off. Well, as I was running, I felt the bushes, so I leapt into the bushes and lay there on my back, happy I was still alive. The shooting started to slow down, and it seemed like I lay there forever. I was so scared and in shock. I started seeing me lying in a casket at home and my family crying as they walked by, except my brother Michael. He just passed by me and put a dime on the side of my casket. I guess he was paying me back for the coke I bought him when I was leaving for Vietnam. Then I realized I wasn't dead, but that the shock was getting best of me, and I was just hallucinating. I must admit I was feeling very alone and abandoned. Then I saw a Vietnamese coming toward me. I thought he was the enemy

He yelled out in broken English, "No, Doc, don't. I am here to help you. He then threw me over his shoulder and carried me, forever it seemed, until we got to where the marines were. Then he handed me over to a big, tall black marine, and then he went back into enemy territory to look for more survivors. He was truly a hero. I owe my life to that man. As the marine continued to carry me down the trail, all I could do was scream and cry how bad it hurt. I must have looked really scary to all the marines I passed by. After a long walk, he laid me down on the ground, and a bunch of corpsman started working on me. I remember how tight they tied the bandages. They gave me morphine, so the pain was not so bad. In fact, I felt pretty good, though I must have been a bloody mess. A helicopter lowered a rope down. They could not land because the enemy was shooting at the helicopter. They tied the rope around me very tightly, and up I went. I was really flying high, if you know what I mean. The crewmen eventually pulled me up and inside the helicopter, and off we flew. Inside were dead and dying marines. It was a nightmare, and blood was everywhere. We headed for the battalion aid station, where they checked my wounds and put me back on a helicopter and sent me to the hospital ship *USS Repose*, which was docked in Da Nang. As I think back now about that experience, well, it gets pretty painful to remember.

I spent a day and a night on the ship. That night I experienced the horror of being strapped very tight into a gurney and eventually rolled into a well-lit room that looked like a surgery room. There was blood and flesh everywhere. The corpsman said they don't have any pain killer. They told me to scream as loud as I could, that it would help. It didn't help at all. They started to debride my wounds with forceps and scalpels. Boy, did it hurt. I even wish I had died back in the bush. When I was done, they put me back on a clean gurney and took me to my bunk, and I fell asleep immediately. I was woken up by the prettiest American red cross worker. I thought I was in heaven. She smiled and gave me a phone so I could call my home in the good ole USA. When I called home, it was very late, and I first woke up my brother Billy. He was so shocked that he almost hung up the phone. I let my family know that I was all right. I was told in the morning that I would be airlifted to a hospital to recover in Japan. Before I was sent out to Japan, I talked to another corpsman I knew who had a minor wound. He told me that a large patrol of my guys was wiped out by the NVA. If I had not been wounded when I was, I would have been on that patrol. I felt horrible. I should have been there to help my marines. When I got to Japan, I was in a lot of pain. I was able to meet my one of my first navy nurses. I knew that I wanted to marry her. She was the most beautiful woman I had ever met, and I told her that. I think she was used to hearing that, though. I spent only a few days in Japan. They took good care of me. Then a short helicopter ride, then I was strapped into a very huge plane, and I was on my way home. I flew home on a stretcher the whole trip. It was no fun, but when I landed at the air base in the USA, I rolled off my stretcher and kissed the ground of America. My dad told me later that when I left for Vietnam he knew that I would either come back in a body bag or a stretcher. I thought my troubles were over, but that was far from the truth.

6
After Vietnam

It was good to be in the USA. I was admitted to the Oaknoll Naval Hospital in Oakland, California, about a two-hour drive from my home. At first I was there for my bullet wounds. I anticipated a quick recovery, then back to Vietnam. I really wanted to go back. Unfortunately, that did not happen. In fact, my hospital stay was over four months. Right away, my wounds got infected. Then even though I was stateside, I came down with falciparum malaria. I got pretty sick while I was there. My fever was so high that they had to cover my whole body in ice to get the fever down, and what a headache I had. The pain was unbearable. My gunshot wounds just wouldn't heal, and infection was spreading. Then I started coming down with different jungle diseases.

One day, I was lying in bed, and my muscles started to tighten up on me. The pain was horrible. My whole body started to cramp up. I guess I went into apoplectic shock. They thought it was a severe reaction to Compazine, which I took to control my nausea from the ongoing malaria. I guess every muscle was closing down on me. That's when they decided to put me in the dying room. Normally, I was in a large ward of about twenty to thirty patients. Because I was so sick, they put me in a private room so I wouldn't die on the ward. They called my dad and told him I probably would not make it through the night. Within a couple of hours, he was there with my bishop to give me a priesthood blessing. All my muscles were in spasm, even my eyelids. They were convinced that my heart would also go. All I could see were some dark shadows moving toward me. My dad told me later that I looked very bad like a scribbled-up old man. They gave me the blessing and told me I would be healed and not die. Both my dad and my bishop said they saw this green light pulsating from my body and it lit up the room. When they left, I felt all my muscles just relax, and I passed out. I woke up the next morning and got out of my bed to see if someone would get me some food. I was really hungry. I wanted to know why I was in the dying room. I felt a little weak but otherwise I felt fine. They were all surprised to see me standing there, and finally, I got some food, and I felt great. Within a few days, all my symptoms were gone—no infected wounds. In fact, they healed so fast that I was left with huge scars. No malaria, no muscle spasms. I was discharged in three days from the time I got the blessing. Another miracle came my way. "Thank you, Lord," was all I can say. When I got discharged from the hospital, I also was discharged from active duty. Now I had to get used to civilian life again. A few months later, I had to go to the Twelfth Naval District headquarters on Treasure Island in uniform to meet a three-star admiral. He awarded me the Silver Star and two Purple Hearts. That's when I learned about what happed to me my last day in the jungle. Years later, I found out that the marine I went to save survived. That brought me great strength. At the ceremony, I felt kind of embarrassed and nervous, but I was proud to be recognized as part of the Marine Corps even if it was only for less than a year.

7
College

After a short time at home, I got my acceptances to Brigham Young University, and off I went to Utah to start college. College was hard work. I signed up for a club that was like a fraternity and sorority. My first assignment was to guard the eternal flame that was by the football field from our archrivals, University of Utah. I guess the night before the football game, students from both universities would try to submarine each other's schools. I borrowed my landlord's truck and drove to the eternal flame to guard it. In a couple of hours, a University of Utah student drove right in front of me and started to run up his engine. So I just rolled down the window and waved. He flipped me the bird and then sped off. An hour later, he came back and did the same thing. He looked like a greaser from the late fifties. He had the right hair, a white T-shirt, and a pack of cigarettes rolled up in his sleeve. I reached back and grabbed the shotgun from the rack. He sped off again, again giving me the bird. He came back another time later. I had enough. I grabbed the shotgun and got out of the truck and started walking toward his car. I could see his scared face in his rearview mirror. Then I just blew out his rear window with rock salt from the shotgun and continued toward him. He tried to peel out but couldn't get his car to move. He turned as white as his T-shirt as I cocked the gun again. His back wheels were just spinning. They finally got a grip and took off like a bat out of hell. He never came back. The rest of my guys ran over to see what happened. I told them what happened while the shotgun barrel was still smoking. They just said, "You are one crazy Vietnam guy." I didn't make it into their club, needless to say.

I lived with a large family in Orem, Utah, while attending BYU. They were really good to me. I became part of their family. One sunny day, one of their sons and I went driving in hills in Provo. I drove a 1967 Plymouth Roadrunner with a Hurst transmission. It was one hot car. It started out sunny outside but quickly turned darker and started to snow. On the way down, the car started to slip and slide. It also started picking up speed, and putting on the brakes only made things worse. Then I suddenly came up to a very sharp turn. I turned the wheel hard to the right. Then for some reason both of us blacked out at the same time. When we woke up, the car was crashed almost head-on into the right side of the mountain. The strange thing was when we got out of the car, we noticed the tire tracks went off the mountain, then came straight back onto the mountain. The Lord was watching over us for sure. During my Christmas vacation, I went home for two weeks. Then I met my then future wife, Cris Garcia, and we had our first date. It was a double date with my brother Ron and his girlfriend. I think I fell in love with Cris at first sight. She is a great person, and she was so beautiful and still is. Cris was born in Havana, Cuba, her father was a very successful importer of hardware goods. Then came Castro and the Bay of Pigs. When Cris was nine years old, her mother, her only sister Gracie (she had no brothers), and she were able to leave Cuba. Her father and the rest of her small family had to stay behind. Only her one aunt was later able to leave Cuba. The rest, she never saw again. I do believe she is one of the bravest women I have ever known. Oh, how I love her.

8
Army

After my winter break, I said good-bye to Cris, and I went back to college. I started having PTSD (post-traumatic stress disorder) problems. Everything was very confusing to me—the terrible nightmares and the night sweats and waking up screaming. I felt like I was going crazy. I had convinced myself that I had to join the army and sign up for the Green Berets. I just wanted to go back to Vietnam. Cris and I dated some more. Then I went and joined the US Army and signed up for the Green Berets. They were scheduling me for combat jump school. I thought I was on the right track to return to Vietnam. I also was in love with Cris, and I had decided to ask her to marry me. While on leave, I asked Cris to marry me while I was practicing baptizing her in our family swimming pool. I proposed at the side of the pool. Lucky for me, she said yes. I told her what my plans were, for me to return to Vietnam as a Green Berets medic. She told me that I was crazy, that I was going back to Vietnam to get myself killed. She wanted nothing of it. At that moment, I realized that I had to make a choice: Vietnam or marry Cris. I did love her so much. I changed my orders from Green Beret to a surgical technology school, which the army had guaranteed me when I signed up. The Green Beret captain was so furious that I thought he was going to shoot me.

Shortly after my decision, Cris and I got married quickly while I was on a short leave. The date was May 30, 1970. I didn't let her graduate or take her to the senior ball. She was hurt but ready to follow me. We got married by the same bishop who gave me the blessing in the hospital. I quickly started surgical technology school instead of the Green Berets. That was part of the deal to get Cris to marry me. She said I just wanted to go back to Vietnam and get myself killed; then she would become a widow. I trained in San Antonio, then finished the OJT training at the Presedeo Army Hospital in San Francisco. Our first real duty station was Fort McClellan, Alabama. I immediately start having PTSD problems, and the nightmares and night sweats would not stop. I would wake up screaming and scare Cris to death.

The army was good to me. I enjoyed my job. It was stressful, but helping doctors operate was exciting. I learned a valuable trade and was pretty good at it. I was promoted to E4. I stayed in the army for a couple years. My time in the army was nothing like the navy—not near as exciting as the navy was. I loved being married to Cris. She was my dream girl. She did a great job supporting me in the army. We also got a chance to be on our own and got closer because of it.

The last six months I was in the army, the PTSD (they didn't have a name for it back then) was getting the best of me. I realized that I wasn't going to make it. I went to mental health clinic, and they agreed with me and decided that I had enough and suggested that I get out of the army before I have to be hospitalized. The army agreed and guaranteed me an honorable discharge. They assured me that I had served my country well and that the Silver Star and two Purple Hearts were proof that I had served my country enough. Still it was a very hard decision. I thought of my wife, who had just got pregnant. I realized it was for the best.

9
Civilian Life

So we left the army and Anniston, Alabama, and traveled across the country in our little Toyota and Cris being a few moths pregnant. We traveled forever, and it was very hot, especially when we crossed the Death Valley desert.

When we reached California, we set up home in a small one-bedroom apartment. I got a job in a hospital as a scrub nurse. I enjoyed my job a lot. I got to scrub in on many types of surgeries. One day, I worked with a couple of orthopedic surgeons. The patient was a daredevil, extraordinary Evil Kin evil. Practically every bone in his body had been broken, including the one we operated on. His right ankle was shattered.

The man had metal throughout his body and enough bolts and screws to open a hardware store. Evil insisted he be awake for his surgeries. He and the surgeon were arguing throughout the surgery. Evil said he only wanted a half-leg cast; and if the doctor, who wanted a full-leg cast, didn't oblige him, he would cut the thing off and beat it over the doctor's head. At that time, he was getting ready to jump a big canyon in Idaho. I asked him if he will make it across. He said, "Hell no, but I need the money." When he left the recovery room, he had two blond bombshells to take him to his room and be his private nurses. He loved to talk, and I love to listen. Another famous surgery was on Flipper the dolphin. That was amazing. We had all kinds of names for the different surgeons. Orthopedics were cowboys, thoracic was chest cracker, and anesthesiologists were all gas passers . While working at that hospital, I did a lot of learning and maturing. It was a good environment to grow.

In the year 1971, my first son was born at the San Mateo Hospital, where I was born at. We drove like maniacs to get to the hospital, and about fifteen minutes later, he was born. His name is Alonzo Prentice Cole IV. We called him Lonnie. He was the cutest baby I ever had seen, a lot better looking than I was. He grew up to be quite a good man. He married a beautiful young woman. She is such a blessing to us all and is a great mother to their five wonderful children.

Well, I decided to go back to college for my AA degree, While I was attending Skyline Junior College, I wrestled for two years and lettered both years. I surely wasn't the best on the team. I lost more than I ever won, but I tried very hard. I remember one match. I was put up against a huge heavyweight. He outweighed me by at least two hundred pounds. My coach—we called him Coach Allen, who was an Olympic coach—advised me, "Whatever you do, don't go for a double-leg takedown. I went for single-leg takedown. I slipped, so I instinctively went for the double-leg. Big mistake on my part. I did take him down, but he fell on top of me. I was on my back. He covered my whole body completely you couldn't tell if I was on my back or on my belly. To add insult to injury, his fat chest was covering my face, and I couldn't breathe at first. I just pinched him to get him off me, but he wouldn't move. I was suffocating under him, so I started biting him, still no movement. Just before *I* was going to black out, I heard the slap on the mat. The referee had given him the pin. It took three guys to roll him off me. I was white as a ghost, and his chest was covered with bite marks. I did have one time I showed my great skill on the mat . I was again wrestling a heavyweight, but this guy was a state champion and all muscle. I was told to not get pinned and we win the match. I was really feeling very sick, but I went out there anyway. I knew I didn't have a chance, but I just had to get it over with. To my surprise, I made to the second round. He did a reversal on me and put me into a pinning combination. All I could hear was my brother Ron. He was yelling, "Don't get pinned." Something snapped in me, and somehow I turned him over onto his back and pinned him. Everyone went crazy on both teams. My surprised opponent just had this shocked look on his face, as if to say, *What just happened here?* I couldn't believe it myself. My team threw me up into the air and started carrying me on their shoulders. At that moment, I just started heaving all over my teammates at first. They didn't even care, but then I started throwing up blood. The next thing I remember I was in a ambulance and on my way to the hospital. They thought I had ruptured my spleen. I spent a week and a half in the hospital. It turned out that that I had a severe case of the Hong Kong flu.

That was the last time I ever wrestled.

One of the saddest times of our lives was when we lost our second son, Brian Phillip Cole. He was born on February 20, 1976. He was born two and a half months early. I saw him in his little crib so tiny and so weak. He fought hard to stay alive but had too many things go wrong. I was working at a mall as a security officer when I got the call. I remember I just started to cry so hard that it physically hurt me. Nothing was ever as painful to me as that day I lost my son. I first went to my dad's house, and together we went to the hospital to tell Cris. It was the hardest thing I ever had to do. My wife, Cris, took it very hard and just started weeping. She was in minor shock. It was such a dark day in the Cole house. My wife continued to take it so very hard. I did all my heavy grieving when we first lost Brian. I had to be strong for my dear wife. The sisters of our church came and stayed with Cris most of the day and evening. There was always some sister there with her. Some were sharing their own painful losses of their children. They remained until Cris was able to get up and do for herself. The only thing that comforted me is that I know I will be able to see and be with my son again. My son Alonzo, as a teenager, wrote a poem for Brian.

The Elegy of Brian

It was the dawn of a new life
He was born into a healthy family
A blessing he could not receive
Complications were stronger to him
The doctors prayed for a miracle
He was the miracle
His mother weary from his birth carried the burden
The child's destiny was apparent
He was born to die
I have never seen anyone live his destiny better
It was a pathetic loss
The spirit held on to make an impression

To proved he had existed
They tried to save the new beginning
Each attempt brought another problem
He was doomed to his destiny
Silently a destiny fulfilled
I was too young to understand
He loved me enough to merely exist
To prove his destiny
To challenge my life and worth
Thank you, my little friend
Your concern is well appreciated
By Alonzo Cole

What a powerful poem written by such a young man who loved his brother so. I just hope my son Brian will not be disappointed in me.

10
Police Years

The next five years of my life were exciting times. Becoming a police officer was a very difficult challenge. I had to take dozens of police written, physical, and oral tests before I was selected by the city of Des Moines. I did very well at the police academy. Still I had so much more to learn as a rookie cop. I remember my first traffic stop, I had him on radar. He was going fifteen miles over the speed limit. I pulled him over and called in the traffic stop. I got out of the patrol car and approached the vehicle and driver very cautiously and asked for his driver's license and vehicle registration. He was very polite and did everything I asked him to do. Then when I got back to the patrol car, I realized I had locked my keys in the patrol car with the lights flashing. I had really goofed up. I called the police station to bring me a set of keys. She said she had the keys but had no way to get them to me. So I was crazy enough to ask the driver if he would drive down to the police station, which was only a few blocks away. He agreed and promptly returned with the keys. I was so much a rookie that after he got back with the keys I still wrote him a ticket for speeding. He looked back at me like I was stupid or something. I guess I was, now that I think of it. I have to admit it wasn't the only time that I locked myself out of my patrol car. The second time, my sergeant and two other police officers responded. I guess this time my sirens were left on, and my portable radio was inside the car, so they thought I was hurt. I have made many hundreds of traffic stops and never repeated locking my keys in the patrol car. In the city of Des Moines, we had several drunk drivers a month. The worst drunk-driving case I ever had was when I caught a driver going fifteen miles per hour in a forty-five-mile-per-hour zone. He was driving all over the road. Added to that, he had no tires on the back of his car. He was driving on his back tire rims. It took me a long time to get him to pull over. When I did get him out of the car to give him a standard field sobriety test, he passed out cold on the road. I had to pull him off so the oncoming traffic would not run over him. I finally got him handcuffed into patrol car backseat. When I got him to the station, he started to wake up. He said the reason he was going so slow was he had a flat tire. He was very surprised when I told him that he had no back tires at all. I tried to give him a field sobriety test, which I couldn't finish. He was so drunk he just couldn't do it.

Then I had him blow into the Breathalyzer, and when he was done, he blew a 3.2. That was so high that he should have been dead. The rest of the night was pretty quiet. Working nights were usually busy until about 3:00 a.m. Then it would get really quiet. One night I got in a foot pursuit of a possible burglar. I chased him forever. Right when I was about to catch him, my gun fell out of my holster. And it took a couple of bounces. Lucky for me, the revolver didn't fire. The suspect got away while I stopped to pick up my revolver. I was pretty lucky, as on the way back to my patrol car, I tripped over the suspect, who was hiding by some trees. I arrested him for alleged burglary. And while I was processing him, his name came up as an illegal alien from Mexico. So the Feds came and picked him up. I know it is a dangerous job, but I only came very close to getting killed twice. The first time was when I had made a routine traffic stop in the residential area of Des Moines. I had two minors in possession of alcohol. When I started back to their car, a still small voice whispered in my ears, *Draw your gun. Danger.* So I backed up to the patrol car and called for backup. Then I told the suspect to drop their keys out of car and to put their hand against the front window where I could see them. I waited for backup to show up and then approached the two kids. It turned out that they had just burglarized a house and stole all of owner's rare wine collection. One of boys had a sawed-off shotgun and was going to use on me when I came back to their car. The one boy broke down and cried, saying, "I'm so sorry, I almost killed you." Another time I almost got killed was when I was dispatched during the day shift to a pharmacy that reported a suspicious person in their area. I got there, and everything looked normal, so I headed for the front door when I heard the still small voice telling me again to *Pull out your gun. Danger.* So I did and approached the front of the pharmacy from the side. It turned out that the armed robber was pointing his gun right at me. He told the pharmacist that he was going to take me out. When he saw me pull out my revolver, he got scared and ran out the back door. We never found him. One night we responded to a home with a suspicious person in the area. I had a reserve officer with me. As we approached the house, we could see no one downstairs. It looked like everyone had vanished. The TV was still on, and there was dinner still on the kitchen table. So we walked to the upper part of house and knocked on the door. Out stepped a very scary lady, her long hair blowing out in the wind. She looked like a freaked-out hippie. She right away responded, "It sure took a long time for you to get here."

She let us inside, and we asked what the problem was. She stated that somebody was in her attic. She pointed toward a large door and told us the people who lived downstairs were druggies and they would come up the stairs, then through the large door, which had a dead bolt in it. I could see nothing to be alarmed about. I was getting ready to leave when I heard a crash in the attic. She screamed, "They're here." I knew I would have to go up the stairs and check it out. I had the other officer stay at the bottom of the stairs, and I started going up, with my revolver and my flashlight in my hands. I slowly went up the stairs. When I got to the top, I heard some crashing sounds again. I was scared. Then I got to the top quickly, and I didn't see anybody, and to my relief, there was a shutter that was flapping in the wind. So I turned around, told the reserve officer, "Everything is all right, so don't shoot me when I come down." At the bottom of the stairs, I talked to the lady and said, "It's all clear up there, but you might need someone to fix the broken shutter." She told us as soon as we leave those hoodlums downstairs will come up the stairs and spy on her. I told her to "Be sure to keep the door locked and also the dead bolt, and I am sure that everything will be okay, but be sure to call us if you have any more problems." That was a very freaky call. By the time we got back to our patrol car, the storm was going full blast. Luckily, she didn't call again.

I took my dad one Saturday night for a drive along. It was a typical Saturday night, busy as all hell. We had a high-speed chase and a dead body in their home, which died from natural causes. But we had to wait there until the coroner showed up. Then I had a couple of traffic stops, and it got quiet until we got a suspicious person at the 7-Eleven store. When we got there, I got out of the car very carefully, told my dad to stay in the car and call for help if I have any problems. I approached the suspect and asked for an ID.

He was extremely nervous and said he had no ID. I told him that I had to pat him down. He looked like he was diffidently on something. When he raised up his arm, I saw what appeared to be something hard and long in his shirt pocket. When I touched him there, he went berserk. He took a swing at me and started to run. I grabbed him by one of his hands and threw him down to the ground. He really put up a big fight while I was trying to handcuff him. My dad showed up at my side, and the suspect tried to slug my dad. Before I knew it, my dad got off three or four punches in on the suspect. They were good punches, and it slowed him down. Help arrived. We got him handcuffed. When we did a total search, we found what appeared to be roll of illegal drugs in his shirt pocket. After later test of the drugs, it was, in fact, illegal drugs. We took him to the Kent jail. When he got locked up, he started screaming, jumping, and pounding on his cell like he was a crazy monkey. Then my dad came in, and he shut up and settled down. He called out to my dad, "Hey, are you FBI?"

My dad just smiled, and I said, "It's okay, Dad."

The prisoner got a little disturbed and yelled, "Oh, he's your dad, I see." After that, he was quiet and peaceful as we finish booking him.

We left, and my shift was almost over, so I dropped my dad off at his car All he said before he drove off was, "Son, I got my money's worth." My dad was one of my best friends. I miss him dearly.

The worst day I ever had was my first and only homicide case as a police officer. A few weeks before the homicide, I responded to an older lady's house. She stated that her son was going to be released from the mental hospital, and she was a little concerned about her safety. I advised her to let us know if she had any trouble to call us. I was concerned about her. When I gave my report, I was told that her son was very crazy. He was arrested before in the act of trying to strangle someone. In World War II, his whole unit was wiped out by the Germans, and he played dead when they went by stabbing the American soldiers. He was stabbed also. Now whenever he saw someone in a uniform, he went crazy. The detective told me not to worry, that he would never get out of the crazy house. I was still worried, so I would patrol her house at least twice a night. A few weeks later, we got another call from her house. It was from her son. He called our dispatch and told her he just killed his mother, then hung up.

We sent three officers to her house. I was the first to arrive, and the house seemed all quiet. My sergeant arrived, and we had one reserve with us. He stayed and covered the front door. My sergeant and I approached the back door, which was unlocked. The sergeant and I entered the house through the back door, with our guns drawn, and started a search of the house by the book. We knew that there were guns in the house and her son was crazy enough to use them. We had searched the kitchen and dining room; *then I entered the living room,* and there she was, lying in an overstuffed chair. Her chest was all bloodied, and she was headless. I quietly told my sergeant on the portable radio. I said, "Sarge, I found her, and I'm sure she's dead, and she is headless." He didn't believe me until he entered the living room. When he saw her, he got very sick. Then he said, "Let's get out of here. We'll call in SWAT." If *the son was still in the house,* it would take a SWAT team to get him out. Well, we called in the SWAT team. They shot in a bunch of teargas grenades. The teargas started a fire, and we had to call in the fire department to put out the house fire. The SWAT team followed right beside the fire department and cleared the house for us to go back in. The son was gone, but we had a homicide for sure.

His mother had, in fact, been decapitated and had dozens of stab wounds in her breast area. It was a really gruesome sight. I spent half the day helping with the investigation, and I had a very large report to write. In police work, you spend more time writing than anything else.

Police work didn't feel the same after that event. Luckily, they captured the son. He was stopped on a simple traffic stop in San Diego, California. He was still wearing the bloody clothes from the night of the murder. The trial went quickly. He was found guilty of murder because of insanity. Hopefully, he is serving a life sentience in the criminally insane ward at Western State Mental Hospital and will never be released.

The police department took a toll on me emotionally. My PTSD symptoms got triggered, which affected my family life. I thought I was calloused to it all, but I wasn't. The worst problem I went through was the politics and religious persecution. I realized that I just couldn't handle it. I made a prayerful decision to resign from the police department.

11
Boeing Years

After I left the police department, I went to work as a security officer for the Boeing Company. I worked there for about five years. I worked as a gate security guard most of the time. What a change of pace it was. I did spend about a year working in plain clothes, with an unmarked car. I would go from one plant to another and cruise the parking lots for any obvious crime. I was busy, and I caught several car prowlers. I cleaned up a prostitution ring in one plant and caught people stealing, doing drugs, and even fornicating in broad daylight. I was very busy guy. Unfortunately, I was doing too good of a job, and executives were reporting that our plainclothes security work was interfering with company production.

The big security boss closed down the operation. I went back to working the gates. I still had some special assignments like security for President Jimmy Carter and other dignitaries. One of my favorite assignments was to guard T. A. Wilson's home. He was the chairman of the board for the whole Boeing Company. On one of the nights, my partner heard strange noises coming from the kitchen. It turned out to be just the ice machine. It was embarrassing when we drew our guns, stormed the kitchen, ready for anything, and all we found was a noisy ice machine. I spent three days and two nights at his house, I got to meet Mr. Wilson and his wife. He was a little quiet, but his wife was very friendly. They lived a simple life in a home that they had for over thirty years. They drove matching Honda Civics until they moved up to Cameros.

As I worked the gates more, I was starting to get bored. I thought I was losing my mind. At night, I would go to VA therapy groups for my PTSD. One day, I was reading the newspaper at work, and it said that over fifty thousand Vietnam veterans had committed suicide. Then I looked at my gun at my side, and maybe I can make it fifty thousand and one. I should have got more help back then. My mind was going crazy from just standing at a gate for eight or more hours. As a gate guard, I still caught employees stealing things from the plant. It meant instant termination to be caught stealing or bringing things into the plants, like drugs and booze. One day while working the day shift at the plant, I was checking lunch pails for any contraband. One guy refused to open his lunch pail. I ordered him to do so. He refused to do so and told me to go screw myself as he walked on by. The next day, he did the same. I talked to my supervisor about it, and he told me next time he does it to grab his Boeing badge and write him up. That was exactly what I did. Two weeks later, he came by my gate, and he was very cooperative. I asked him why the change. He politely told me that the only way he could get a day off from work was to get a guard mad enough to write him up. I guess he had been working seven days a week with overtime for over nine months.

Boeing liked me and even wanted to make me a supervisor, but the job was too stressful, and the pay was less.

I started a part-time business with my little brother Mike. The business grew very fast. I eventually had to make a decision whether to stay at Boeing, making far more than I ever did as a police officer, or grow my new company. I chose to quit Boeing and give our little business full-time attention.

During the Boeing years, our little girl Heidi was born on March 31, 1978. She was a jewel and brought great joy to our little family's life. She still is the prettiest little girl I know. She is now married to a great man who works as a firefighter and is a major in the National Guard. He has deployed many times for our country. We are all very proud of the service he gives our country. They now have four little ones of their own. When Heidi was born, it was such a blessing. We had lost our second son to a premature birth. It almost killed my wife and me and was very hard on our son. I don't think I ever cried so hard as I did the night we lost Brian. Now Heidi was born, and we could have the joy of taking our baby home again, but that was not to be. Heidi was sick with jaundice, and she would have to stay in the hospital for a few more days. I didn't have the courage to tell my wife. So I went straight home from my visit of Heidi. I called in sick at work that day. I stayed home and prayed and fasted all day. That evening, the Lord revealed to me that everything would be okay. I went back to the doctor and said my baby is going home with her mother and me. The doctor said, "You are right, Mr. Cole. Your daughter is no longer sick, and her jaundice is gone." Then I went to see my wife, and I gave her the good news. Of course, she already knew.

Two years later, we dedicated our son Brian's grave. It was probably the most peaceful time of my life. Brian lived a very short life, but he left a powerful impression on our souls. I remember my two-year-old daughter, Heidi, saying, "I am going to miss my brother Brian."

12
My First Business

Now running a small business with my brother, that was stressful.

The business of Office Interior Care grew very fast. We got a contract for the US government in Washington, Oregon, and Idaho. That work caused our company to grow quite fast. By our second year, we had eight employees. Our business was doing electrostatic painting in the office and other metal furniture.

We also built desktops from our own woodshop. We grew too fast, and my brother and I didn't see eye to eye on practically every part of the company. I was in charge of sales and finances. My brother managed the production, which would always cost more than our sales would bring in. He was a man who only new quality in every job he did. All the good credit I had was being swallowed up by OIC. We had some great experiences during our OIC years. I remember one trip in Oregon for the National Parks Department. One of my employees was taking the trash out to the dipsy dumpster. He got chased away by a very big and angry bear. You should have seen the look on his face when he came back. One day, we decided to have employee-of-the-month awards. We gave the employee who won a new colored TV set a VCR and some cool movies. Our employee was so proud I thought he was going to cry. A week later, I got a call from one of my customers in Oregon. He said that our head employee had a breakdown and I better get over there as quick as I could. I drove for three hours. I found him sitting on the floor, crying like a baby. His girlfriend had left him and ran off with the TV and VCR. I had to talk to him for hours just to get him up from the floor.

A few months later, we got notified that we had won an Award of Excellence from the federal government. They insisted we receive the award in Washington, DC. We had to pay for the trip of course.

My brother and I took our sons with us. It was quite a trip, especially when I got to go to the Vietnam war memorial. It had a very strong impact on me as I saw the names of so many marines I knew. It was like it opened my wounds again. But now they were in my mind.

My PTSD started to return again. Maybe it was always there. We also had President Reagan speak to us. He told us that small businesses were the backbone of America. Washington, DC, was amazing in so many ways. I wish all Americans could go there. I also saw so many homeless and very poor people on the streets. It was a hard and a strange paradox.

OIC lasted about five years. Then my brother and I went our own ways. I still had OIC but without my brother. I was on my own, and my wife was such a great support. I moved into a smaller place and started to subcontract the services I provided.

I was heavily in debt and struggling to stay afloat. Then my brother started to submarine me by going to our customers and telling them that he was the backbone of our business and would offer to do the work cheaper. He was always playing with my mind, and after a year, I had a nervous breakdown. We were in some pretty dark and painful days, and I had to file for bankruptcy for the business. OIC was no more.

13
Second Business

I had to scramble to earn enough to pay my personal bills. I just broke down physically and mentally. I remember being so depressed I sat out on my porch and tried willing my heart to stop that way I would die of natural causes. I was a broken man. Finally, I had to give up everything and file personal bankruptcy. I felt like a failure to my family and all I knew. We lost our home, and I put our stuff in storage. We moved in with my wife's sister and her family in Southern California. We were dirt broke, and I was mentally and physically broken also. But life went on. We were still a family. We had a roof over our head and food to eat, and our children did well in their new schools. I started another small business and, in a few months, with my nephew and my brother-in-law's help. It started turning a very small profit so we could afford to move in to our own place. I will never forget all the help Cris's family was to us.

I had two additional breakdowns while still in Southern California. The first one, I ended up in the hospital for a week. I had a blood pressure of 325/155 and rising. The doctor said I should not be alive. The nurses wouldn't even look me in the eye when they came in to treat me. I called up my family and said my good byes. I knew when I fell asleep I would wake up in heaven. Some how the doctors were able to reverse my high blood pressure, and again I beat death's cold embrace.

The next time, I ended up in the intensive care. I had just given up on myself. I felt like I just couldn't go on anymore. I had lost all will to live. That night I was visited by a man dressed in white, and he seemed to glow. He looked a little familiar. He came to the head of my bed and started to talk to me. He told me, "Do you know what your problem is?"

I thought, H*ow could he know all my problems?* Then I knew for some reason he did know all my problems. He continued to say that I have been trying to carry all my burdens by myself. He reminded me that I am not alone, that the Lord is always with me, and that he can help me if I just let him in again. Something changed in me that night. I really felt his spirit and that I was not alone and that the Lord is ready when I am. He reminded me that the Lord loves me. He then walked out of the ICU. Many people said I was visited by an angel. I know he was real and that night changed my life. I got out of the hospital that morning and started to move forward. I realized that I had made a serious error in leaving Washington. The only thing that seemed normal to me was the church we went to. We were accepted and put to work. My family was ready for me to get my act together. After that experience in the hospital, I realized it was time for us to move back to Washington. Again I must say that my wife and I will always be thankful for all the help my wife's sister Gracie and her family gave us in our time of need.

We moved back to Washington and into a town house in Federal Way, Washington. Members from our church were waiting to help us unpack, and they took right over. They helped us feel welcome and glad to be home. I had no job and only enough money to live for two months, but we were glad to be back at home. The Lord blessed us, and I found a job in one month, working for an office furniture company in Seattle. I ran the furniture services for the company. I was doing well there. We were making headway. Then the owner's daughter started working with us, and she had her eye on my job. After about three years, I quit and started a new company called Commercial Services and Consultants Inc. CSC I didn't have much money, so I had my subcontractors pay me for the work I brought in to them. Then I went to work for my old boss as a subcontractor. In other woods, I was the middleman. I built the company up slowly, and eventually I had enough profit that I could give myself a decent salary. At last I could make a decent living for my family. We lived in a nice townhome on a small private lake. The complex had a swimming pool, which my daughter and I used quite often. My son was a senior in high school and preparing himself for college for a year, then a full time mission for our church. Life was on a roller coaster. But we were surviving, and the company grew from two employees to eight employees. Our success was due to keeping out of debt. At first it was easy to do, but as the company grew, debt started creeping in, which later in time became a fatal error. By the time my son had finished his mission (he served two years in Northern Italy) and finished his college, the business was growing really fast. My son approached me and stated he wanted to come to work for me. It was his idea, and I was proud to have him. I think our key employee felt a little threatened by my son. He resigned shortly after bringing Alonzo aboard. He was one of the best employees I ever had. I know he will be a great success in life. Now our company was growing too fast. In one year, we did over a million dollars in sales. I now had no time for mental problems like PTSD. It went underground, you might say. I buried myself in my business and did volunteer work for our church. I really enjoyed working with the youth of our church. We have been blessed with a royal generation of young ones.

I did a lot of volunteer work with the Boy Scouts of America and helped out as a Wood Badge staff member. On the way to a training session, I had a very faith-promoting experience. As I was driving, I noticed on the opposite side of the road a serious car accident. There was only one car involved. It must have just happened, because it was upsid down and smoking. When I got to the car, I noticed there was a young girl trapped in the driver's seat. She was hurt and really screaming, "Help me!" I tried to open the door to get her out. It wouldn't budge no matter how hard I pulled on it. There was no one to help me. I prayed that I could just open the door. Then suddenly a tall thin man with long black hair showed up. He looked familiar. He motioned me to help him lift on the car. I did, and then, to my surprise, the car turned completely over and back on to its wheels. The door on the driver's side just popped open, and I was able to get the injured girl out of the car. *What had just happened?* I thought. As I started giving first aid to the young driver, I looked for the man, but he was gone. The young girl was starting to go into shock, so I turned my attention back to her. She had some minor cuts and scrapes but otherwise was okay. I got her to slow down her breathing and got her to calm down. I told her that she was going to be okay. I looked back at the car, and it was still smoldering. Suddenly, people started to show up to help from everywhere. They were creating a panic and scaring the injured girl. I had to calm them down also. I was surprised how quick the fire department showed up. They took care of the car and took over with the young girl. I knew she was in good hands, so I just left. When I told my fellow Wood Badgers what had happened to me, All they could say was that God works in mysterious ways. This is so very true.

My business was steadily growing. It had been for years, and I'm sorry to say so was the debt. Then the stress of the business started to affect my health. I took a dive for the worst. I was under tremendous stress and started having heart problems. I had to have two stents placed in my heart (later, I got a pacemaker in my heart), and I had several major surgeries. I had a big surge of work, which my son took the lead until I was allowed to go back to work. Then they discovered I had a tumor in my pituitary gland, at the base of my brain. It was small but had a huge impact on my body. I had to have two surgeries to cure the problem. One was done by a brain surgeon. He went through my nose into my brain and removed most of the tumor. While I was recovering, I almost died from Diabetes Insipidus.

The other procedure was called a Gamma Knife. It was grueling. They had to drill clamps into my skull so that I would not move my head at all. It was tough. It took over one grueling hour to finish. They used highly concentrated radiation to kill the remaining part of the tumor. While all this was going on, my wife and son were running the business. Then I made a fatal mistake, when I started feeling better, of opening another store. At the same time. A major and key employee quit because everything was getting messed up and was too unorganized. The main store was being neglected. I guess I just bit off more than I could chew. I also learned not to borrow money to pay your general overhead. It was my fault. I have learned you need to keep the size of your company at the size that you are capable to manage. Total office interiors.(TOI) took a steep dive when we closed down the second store. I was still having medical problems. The company and I almost collapsed. We got through the mess but with too much debt. Alonzo took charge of the company, and I worked as a salesman for my son. The horrible truth was I was getting tired of the fast pace of business. I needed to slow down.

Then something new came into the picture. That was when my daughter wanted to start a business with me as her partner. I said I would do it part time because I worked for my son also. That only lasted for a few months, and again I started another company called Heidi Grace

Design with Heidi. Alonzo took over TOI completely. I now regret that decision, but my son never complained. Now I was going full steam ahead with Heidi Grace Designs. I told Heidi I will give my all for three years; then I am finished. Either someone can buy my 50 percent or we can sell the whole company. So now I'm involved with my fourth company.

14
Heidi Grace Designs

Things really started to get busy right away.

Before I started working with my daughter, Heidi my wife and I took a trip to Mexico with some friends. The whole trip was a comedy of errors. When we landed, I forgot my carry-on bag that had our money and passports. I had to run past the guards and to the tarmac and chase down the plane. They stopped the plane for me, and a flight attendant brought me my bag. Then a few days into the trip, I had a seizure and passed out and hit my head. Two days later, I went body surfing, and I got caught in a riptide. I forgot that I was supposed to swim sideways. I just headed for the beach. It seemed so close, and the riptide just pulled me out deeper. I was being sucked underwater, and all I could do was try to swim back to the surface for a breath; then I went down under again. I was getting weaker and didn't think I was going to make it. I thought, W*hat a horrible way and place to die.* I ask the Lord to help me. I fought myself to the surface, knowing this was my last time before I would go under for good. Then to my surprise a little Mexican boy like an angel came floating by me on a small inner tube. I grabbed on to his little inner tube and hung on for dear life. Then a man in a motorboat must have seen my predicament. He moved his boat toward me. I clamped on to the side of his boat and let go of the inner tube. He towed me back to the shore. I must have lay there for several minutes. I had no strength to even get to my knees. The amazing thing was Dennis, my friend, had come out to save me, and he got trapped in the undertow. He was holding on to the other side of the boat, so we both got towed in. Not as tired as I was, he walked over to me and helped me up to my feet. He said, "Lon, I thought I was going to lose you then I got caught in the undertow myself, and all I could do was fight to stay afloat When we made it back to the resort swimming pool, I told my wife. All she could say was, "You're just trying to pull my leg. No way did you almost drown." I decided to go back to my room to get some rest. When I got there, I could see out the balcony to where I was swimming. It was only about fifteen to twenty feet from the shore. Then it hit me what had just happened, how close I was to dying, and I fell on the bed and just wept for a long time. Mexico had one more surprise for me on the day before we were to leave. We went to a resort where they filmed the movie *Predator* with Arnold Schwarzenegger. It was beautiful, and I dove off the rocks into the cool water, then had dinner by the waterside. Unfortunately, I sampled some of the local tortillas with my meal. The next day, as we were getting ready to leave, I got very sick. When we got to the airport, I gave my carry-on bag to my wife. I went to camp out in the bathroom, I lost all track of time. When I got up, I was so dizzy I couldn't see where I was going. Someone pointed me in the direction of the departure gate, and I staggered toward the gate. I looked for my passport and tickets, but I realized my wife had my bag. Then I looked up and saw my wife running toward me, with my ticket and passport in hand. I think she said "Hurry up the plane is leaving." I pushed myself past the gate people and custom agents. (I was to numb to care)who were armed by the way. I made it to my wife, but the custom people started to pull me back. Then speaking in Spanish, my Cuban wife must have explained to them what was going on. They let go, and we ran to the gate and begged them to open the door so we could get on the plane. They finally consented, and we were escorted to first-class seats. That wasn't the end because for the whole flight back, I was so sick that I ended up flying toilet-class instead of first-class. I couldn't eat any of the fancy food. I remained sick for days after I got home.

Another thing that I did before I started working for HGD while I was growing OIC my second company was I bought a building. I got it for a great price. The seller was an old Vietnam veteran like me and a marine tunnel rat. The building was my major investment for the future. In the later years, it turned out to be the one thing that drove us into terrible financial mess. I poured tens of thousands of dollars into the building to keep from losing it, only to have it taken by the bank. Anyway what a mess I created again.

But let's get back to HGD and my daughter, who by the way is one of the most talented and a natural artist I have ever met. At first it was pretty exciting. We traveled to Taiwan and all over the United States. I started to get my own fan club and acquired the title of "Scrap Daddy." It was a weird experience for me, because I had never work in an industry that was composed of ninty-nine percent women. I learned the power of estrogen. I got along pretty well. Let me tell you, women can be great business owners and tough when they need to be. It was hard and very tiring work, but we were doing pretty good. We had some great and very loyal employees who helped us grow. About the second year in, I had to borrow money to make our overhead cost. That was a big mistake. You would think I should have had learned my lesson, considering the mistakes I have done before. We also got our inventory way up from the product that we imported from Taiwan. Somebody had double ordered it. Now we are in deep trouble. At the end of our third year I was really tired and ready to close down the company. Heidi was becoming quite a celebrity in the scrapbook world. Our company had a great image also. We traveled across the country to promote Heidi and the company. People loved her and our products. That's when a company contacted us and offered to buy the company out right for over one million dollars. We sold the company to them and paid off most of our debt (we should have paid all of our debt). We were left with about a two-hundred-thousand dollar profit, which we split, between Heidi and myself. Of course, that was before taxes. We paid all of that. Always pay your taxes no matter what. That was the first time I closed down a business and made a little profit. Heidi went to work for the company who bought us and was making a good income and was traveling all over the world. She was famous and still is. I went back to work for Alonzo, my son. He was a pleasure to work with. He is a hard worker, and he is very frugal and patient.

15
PTSD Years

Things started to slow down for me, and life seemed easy. I had always been a high-stress-job kind of guy. It's like I kind of lost interest in life again. Inside I was changing. It started back when 911 happened. What an impact that event had on me and the world. I started having nightmares again. I was dreaming that I was being chased by some dark evil force that meant me great harm. They were always so very close to getting me. Then I would wake up exhausted and really terrified for hours.

At the same time, I worried about everything going on around me. I was having really strange thoughts and started to become hypervigilant about the nighttime. I would lie in my bed and figure how the bad guys would break in and how I would have to stop them. I was up prowling my house, looking for someone who meant me harm. My feelings and thoughts I kept to myself. My wife had no idea this was going on. She new something wasn't right, though. As years passed by, my secret problems were getting worse.

We were enjoying our new home, and I was working very hard in our church with the youth, which I really enjoyed. As my job and work was slowing down, I started struggling with my old PTSD problems, and I was getting very little sleep. This went on for a couple of years. I knew I needed to get some help, but I didn't want to burden my family, especially my wife, who was caring a heavy load for herself. I started having heart problems again. My physical body was a wreck. My mental health was starting to slip very fast.

At the end of 2007, something snapped in me. The dreams I had would continue on during the day. I had these horrible thoughts of hurting the ones I loved and myself. I tried to keep my thoughts locked inside of me. I felt I was going to explode. I knew I had to get help. I told my wife what I was thinking and all the other things that was going on inside of me. She got scared and drove me to the VA hospital. I talked to my regular doctor, and what I was thinking started to come out He became concerned about me and recommended that I see a VA psychiatrist. Well, we went home, and the next day I woke up and started hearing things that were not there. Then my body started to shut down. My wife took me to see the VA psychiatrist. He immediately admitted me to the lockdown mental ward, where I spent three weeks. It was the darkest time of my life, next to losing Brian. I don't remember much. There was a lot of medication and emotional ups and downs. The nurses and doctors really helped me, though. I was diagnosed with OCD, PTSD and major depression. I was a mess, and they had me on some pretty heavy medicines. I was very suicidal. After three weeks, things were starting to make sense. While I was in the ward, I wrote a poem about my time in the ward. It's called Saints and Warriors. The warriors are the patients, and the saints are the caregivers.

Saints and Warriors

Wrapped together both warriors and saints
Locked into a challenge to give and receive
Sometimes it's hard to take it all in
As the battle rages all hope they will win
No fanfare in victory their service so subtle
Success sometimes denied the team shares the pain
As a new warrior arrives the saints rally again
Day after day the drama's the same
The names are forgotten their hurting remains
Warriors in foxholes fighting to survive
Saints are all praying that the warriors will last
Who is the hero the warriors or saints
All get the medal the work is the same
Warriors fight for freedom saints ease their pain

While in the lock-down ward, I would come up with all kinds of schemes to kill myself. One was to figure a way to overdose. Thanks to the vigilance of the doctors and nurses, that plan didn't work. Another plan was to jump the fence and swim out in the lake so far that I could not make it back and I would drown. I remember before I was admitted I tried to drive my car into an embankment. I swerved just before I hit it.

The turning point for me, though, was on Christmas eve. In 2007 I tried to go to sleep, but I was thinking that all was lost. I couldn't stop crying. I was so alone, and I felt like no one cared. The VA brought me some little presents, but I didn't care about anything. Later because of all the pills I took I fell asleep. That morning, when I woke up, I had warm socks on me and a beautiful handmade quilt covering me. I felt so warm I was sure an angel had brought them. Something had changed in me. I felt hope and the love of my family, and I knew that I can beat this. When my attitude started to change, so did my path to wellness. I was ready to move on. From the mental health ward, I was transferred to a PTSD Dom where I spent sixweeks, but I could go home on weekends. The Dom consisted of intensive one-to-one, and group therapy. When I had finished all this treatment, I started to get a handle on things. I still had the negative thoughts, but I had no urges to act on them. To this day, I sometimes have the negative thoughts, and I have been taught that we all have those experiences. Now I know not to ponder on them. Following my treatment, the VA ascertained that I couldn't handle stress of daily work. I had to quit working. I still tried to go into work for a while, but halfway through the day, I would become very anxious about everything. All my adult life I had been a hard worker; I loved to work. Now my life had changed, and I had to change with it. I have had a few relapses and had to be admitted to a mental health unit a couple of additional times. So life became different. I had to avoid all stress if possible. Throughout my life I have been in high-stress jobs. Now I have to live and avoid stressful things like a plague.

I still suffer from PTSD, OCD, and depression, but I think I have got a better control of things now though it is a struggle. I have a great support system through the VA. I get great mental health care. So my life had to change. The stigma of these diseases, I hope, will change in people's hearts and minds. The strange thing about PTSD was that I had problems, but I didn't notice it. I guess it has bothered me ever since Vietnam. My wife always noticed it. It would cause a lot of arguments. To this day, I don't know how my wife put up with me or still does.

I noticed I was forgetting things regularly, and I was becoming very reclusive at home. I can't handle crowds or too much excitement. My wife said that I always had a memory problem, but I knew it was getting worse. I would start forgetting where I was or why I went there or how I got there all the time. I would forget whom I was talking to on the phone and why I called or what I wanted to say. I had trouble remembering what to say when I was trying to explain things. It was very annoying and challenging.

16
Dementia

About a year passed by. The VA gave me some great help. I continued to attend group therapy sessions and one-to-one session with a psychologist and a psychiatrist, and there was medicine to help me. I was not alone. I had my wife, my family, friends, my faith, and the VA; and I knew the Lord was with me. Then the VA gave me some very detailed test for my memory.

When I came back to get the results, I told the doctor an Alzheimer's joke, about a guy who went to see his doctor and the doctor told him, "I have some bad news for you."

"What is that?" the patient asked.

"Well," the doctor said, "you have cancer."

"That's horrible," said the patient.

Then the doctor said, "I have worse news for you."

"What is that?" the patient again asked.

Then the doctor said." "You also have Alzheimer's."

The patient answered, "Well at least, I don't have cancer."

My doctor didn't laugh, and that's when he gave me the bad news that I had scored very low on all the tests, saying we are pretty sure that you do have early on-set Alzheimer's.

Well, all I could say was, "At least I don't have cancer."Then he started to laugh. When we left the doctor's office, I asked my wife, Cris, what's her take on all of this. She said sadly, "I was hoping you would get a pass on this one." I now started to realize how serious this was, but I kept it to myself for a while. I started going through the grieving side of being told that I have Alzheimer's. Then I remembered what the doctor told me. He said, "Try to get a hold of the Alzheimer's Association. They can be a great help to you."

So I called them. (They have a 24/7 phone number, 1-800-272-3900.) I called at two o'clock in the morning, and I got a real person to talk to. I showered her with so many questions, and she answered all my questions. She started me on a journey that I will be on for the rest of my life. I knew again that I was not alone. I have the Lord, my wife, my family, my faith, and the Alzheimer's Association; they all have got my back. I started and now attend three support groups, and volunteer as an adviser for the Alzheimer's Association. I have been asked to speak and read my poems to many groups of people. I still tell my Alzheimer's joke to anyone who will listen to me. I love to see people laugh. Would I like see a cure for Alzheimer's? You bet I would, and someday it will come, and I will be ready. It's been close to six years now since my diagnosis, and my memory is getting worse. My disease is progressing slowly, which is good because it gives me more time with my family and more time to do something with my life. We need to use the time God gives us wisely. It's getting harder for me to write. I make several mistakes, and I have to go back often to correct them. I am no longer outgoing like I was before. I don't drive anymore. That was one of hardest joys I had to give up. It's like losing your independence. I have problems communicating, and I have times when my brain shuts down on me. I am starting to have Parkinsons symptoms, like a lot of shaking and impaired balance and sleep disorders. They suspect that I also have Lewy body dementia, but I am surviving. Still I write poetry. I have published two books of poetry, and now this book. I know that my family will have a lot of pressure dealing with me and my problems as my disease progresses. I pray we can all get through it. I know the day will come when I won't remember anything. I'm living for today, and I may have Alzheimer's, but Alzheimer's does not have me. I know that it's a horrible disease and the day will come when I won't recognize even my family, and experience much worse problems than that. That's why I'm writing this book now before I forget how to do so. I am very blessed with a very supportive family. I know it will be harder on them in the future. As the disease progresses, I will realize less what is going on with myself. The word for that symptom is *Anosognosia*, where I don't realize how sick I really am. For that may turn out to be a blessin g. I hope and pray I will not become combative, angry, and aggressive. I am staying very active in volunteering with the church and the Alzheimer's Association. You need to keep your mind active and exercise often, and eat healthy foods. What you put in your body eventually ends up in your brain. Exercise your brain often. Give it a workout, and always stay active and positive. Don't let yourself get depressed. I plan to stay in the early stage for as long as the Lord will allow me. I learned that there is one advantage of having dementia and Alzheimer's. That is that you get to hide your own Easter eggs and Christmas presents. Did I say have humor? Well, I love humor. It really helps.

In 2013, the Alzheimer's Association asked me to get in touch with a reporter named John Sharify from KING 5 News, out of Seattle, which I did. He and an excellent photojournalist named Doug Burgess did a short documentary about me and having Alzheimer's. Less than two months later, it was on television. The segment won an Emmy award for best story. John, also with Doug, won the Edward R. Murrow Award. At the Emmy Awards night, he awarded me the Emmy he won for best story. He told me that I earned it. That was a proud moment.

My journey through dementia has been quite a journey. I started writing poetry again. It became my passion, and helps keep my mind active. Thanks to the help of John Sharify and many others, I got my first book of poetry published, which is entitled *You Are Not Alone: Poems of Hope and Faith* in April 2013. About a year later, I started my second book of inspirational poetry, which is entitled *Alive and Thankful: Life Is a Gift*. It was self-published in November 2014.

I learned a few things about writing books. Writing the book is the easy part. Promoting and selling the book is really the hardest work of all.

And that's what I have been doing for over a year now. My dementia is starting to creep in, but I won't let it slow me down.

Now I do presentations and, book signings and readings at care facilities, senior centers, libraries, military bases, and bookstores with the help of my wife and friends. I try to be very active, and I love to meet people. Of course, my wife and friends have become my drivers. Remember this; Winston Churchill said "Never, never, never, never give up."

17
Conclusion

It was once said to me by a doctor that he had never met a patient with so many serious medical conditions as I had. Many of those conditions are life threatening, some life ending. I have knocked on death's door too many times in my life. So what about celebrating survival? What does that mean? I look at life as a precious gift from God. We must be grateful and celebrate every moment God has given us. Things can get really rough in life, but there is always something to learn from those trials. I have had many faith-promoting stories in my life. Faith is very important to me. It is my foundation and helps me to have hope and gives me strength. Life is meant to be lived. Though I have faced death so many times, I still value the life that God has given me. That's why I am "Alive and Thankful." Just being alive is not enough. You must learn and practice being thankful for what God has given you. I had some fairly dark days in my life as a young man and as an adult. The Lord I know was and is with me, and even a few guardian angels. I have always tried to keep the faith. The spirit is in all of us, and it counts the most. The spirit is eternal. It existed before you were born. It will move on with you into eternity. Death is not the end but a continuation of life at its best. I love life, and all it offers me, both the good and the bad though I prefer the good if I get the choice. I learned many lessons over the past years. I learned that God comes first, then family, your religion, and then your service to others. I value all the lessons I have learned in life.

I learned what not to do in business, and I learned how to be a success in business. I learned that life isn't always going be a great success story, but there will be many small victories that can be just as rewarding as the big successes. Most of all, I learned that all the effort we give is good, and necessary to achieve happiness and lasting peace. "We weren't sent here to fail."

That is not the Lord's way.

I am truly a blessed child of God. I have a wonderful family, good friends, and a tremendous faith in the Lord Jesus Christ. I also have a good knowledge of what lies ahead for me. I pray we will all be united in one purpose that is, to be together with those we love and our Heavenly Father for eternity.

Thank you.

Camping trip age ten   **Enlisted in the Navy age 17**

Boot Camp

**Cris And Lon
Police Years**

Vietnam

Celebrate Survival

There all kinds of problems that drag us down
But there is always a way to turn them around

We live to be happy being happy helps us live
But there is no true happiness until you learn how to give

Discouragement is a word that we must learn how to fight
The opposite is accomplishment which is doing what"s right

So celebrate survival in the best way you can
And honor all of life because living is grand

Be fierce in your battle in doing what is good
Don"t waste your time or energy being misunderstood

Be alive and be thankful for all you can be
Count your blessings be glad that you are free

You Rock My Life

The love I have for you
Is much deeper than snow
It permeates my body
And warms my soul

All these years
You have stayed close to me
Our marriage is constant
For all of eternity

You are my life
As we share equal space
I see a pureness
as I look into your face

I thank the Lord
Each and every day
I light up inside
As you're coming my way

You have given me children
Who opened my heart
That I have felt pride
From the very start

I knew that I loved you
From the first time we met
You rock my life
I will never forget

You're Not on Your Own

Ever wondered why you don't fit
Or don't belong to a special clique
Why can't other people remember your name
It seems so unfair and such a shame

Why do you leave when you really should stay
Does depression plague you in a haunting way
It's hard to believe that no one cares
That you're on your own with no one to share

How do you fight the desire to be down
Do you live to be lonely void of all sound
Oh what an empty place you are in
No matter what you do it seems you can never win

Now the darkness surrounds you wherver you go
It is so painful right down in your soul
Why cry out for help there is no one to care
Have you lost all your hope is life so unfair

You must find some hope before it's too late
Drop to your knees there's no time to wait
Call to the Lord as loud as you can
Plead for his mercy he will understand

Depression can take you beware of its sting
The dark one wants you to throw in the ring
Hold on tight the ride may be rough
With the Lord on your side nothing is too tough

The light may feel further than you want to go
That's all an illusion you can reach the goal

Trust in the Lord he wants you to prevail
You are not on this earth to constantly fall or fail

Now is the time to choose what is right
You must hold on to God's hand and be willing to fight
All of your troubles will never be gone
Your walk with the Lord will help you move on

You're Not Alone

I have been told that you're not alone
I wish it was always that way
So often it seems you're all on your own
They leave when you want them to stay

You search for the right answers
But even the questions are gone
You rest for a moment or two
But all your worries still move on

The quest it seems so shallow
As the victory is slipping away
Solutions they are too hollow
There is darkness even at day

I am not afraid to face it
I must do the best that I can
And if I fall short in my journey
I will get up and start again

You're Looking at the Best

There are some people that always rise to the top
They have the drive and determination not to stop

They're constantly moving you won't see them rest
One thing you know you're looking at the best

These are achievers in the highest degree
They get things done that we can't even see

We need people like them for our world to go
To prove to the rest of us there's so much to know

I'm proud to be counted as one of their friends
I've got their back and I won't give in

They're usually well-known but not everyone
They're working so hard while others have fun

They're go-getters from the very start
All that they do comes from the heart

I thank them so much for what they have done for us all
They help us stand tall when we are feeling so small

WW-ll Vets

They fought for their lives
And our lives too
They laid it on the line
For me and for you

Now that they're leaving
Their memory is true
We owe so much
To the Vets of WW-ll

They did their job well
And saved us all
We would be in a mess
But they answered the call

Our personal freedom
Would have been lost
Yet they paid the price
And they suffered the cost

Now most are in heaven
They're on the Lord's side
Just waiting for us
With their arms open wide

Why We Have Pain

Pain is such an awful feeling no matter who you are
It's not a pleasant experience whether close or even far

One thing is for sure you want it to stop, how much can you
endure?
It truly is a burden that you hope to find a cure

To make it stop or go away you will do what you have to do
Pain seems never ending. It always a bother to you

When will it stop! I finally shout, Will it ever end?
Constant pain is a torture for it comes again and again

There are many types of pain that I wish would go away
Emotional pain is an awful plight. No wants it to stay

Spiritual pain is the worst: it can linger all through your life
It can drag you down into darkness and cut through you like a
knife

Pain has lots of friends that no one wants to see
Like guilt, shame, worry, and fear for misery loves company

No one is free from pain there is a reason that it exists
The opposite of pain is the pure love of joy we wouldn't want to
miss

Joy comes from God it will always be there
He loves us more than we ever can know and shows us that he
cares

Where Do We Go

Sometimes our memories come and go
They pass through our mind fast and slow

We try to hold them as tight as we can
We end up confused and don't understand

Where did they go? Why are they gone?
Will they come back, or have they moved on?

Most memories we lose are short-term I'm told
It usually happens when we start getting old

"I can't remember" is a familiar phrase
Our minds end up in a dark misty maze

It's happening more often I'm afraid to say
We seem to forget something every day

Where do we go to get help that we need
Someone that's wiser than me I concede

Whoever we find must really care
They must have my trust and be willing to share

When Warriors Get Old

What do you do when a warrior gets old
The stories they could share that have never been told

Someday they will die like we all will
I hope that their memory will stay close to you

They gave it their all and sometimes even more
So we could enjoy peace from shore to shore

The warriors are needed so we can stay free
They did it for you and they did it for me

I was a warrior and that makes me proud
I'm glad that I served and I'll shout it out loud

So when you see a warrior show them you care
Then when you need warriors they will sure be there

What Joy I Have

I see him only in the pictures
But I know he always is near
And when I really need him
He's there to erase all my fears

He brings me strength and joy
I feel his love each day
He lifts me from the shadows
And hears me when I pray

When I feel so lonely
I know that he'll be there
To surround me with his awesome love
He shows that he truly cares

He sacrifices so much for us
We can never repay the debt
He took upon him the sins of all
In the garden as he wept

The day will come I truly hope
When I can feel his loving embrace
What joy that I will have
As I meet him face-to-face

Now he reigns in great power
At his Father's side
To intervene in our behalf
With his arms open wide

What Is a Patriot

What is a patriot in these latter days
Is it someone that lives to be free
Or is freedom a product we don't have to earn
It's just like taking whatever we see

I think a patriot is a rare breed
Someone willing to take on the wrong
They're not afraid to face their foes
They stand tall, wise, and strong

A patriot is someone that does what they can
Because freedom requires hard work
Sacrifice comes as part of the plan
When called on they will not shirk

They're not the most popular
Or famous that you know
But when asked to serve
They're the first ones to go

We need more patriots
That is for sure
That are willing to give
And not afraid to endure

I call out to all of you
It's time to carry on
If we're not careful
Our freedoms will be gone

We Owe So Much to You

There is a group of people
Who show the world they care
They put their best foot forward
For young ones everywhere

It's not easy to be teacher
Or measure their service and work
And when others try to put them down
It can drive me to go berserk

They have a special purpose
In the lives of all our youth
And when it's time to help us learn
They can teach us right and truth

Where would we be in our lives
If teachers didn't care
The lessons we would never learn
Now that seems so unfair

Not every teacher can be the best
But most are true and real
There's more to teaching than just the class
What you learn affects how you feel

So when you meet a teacher
Tell them thank you for all they do
And if you are a teacher
We owe so much to you

We Are the Stewards

We are the stewards of the world we share
And sometimes forget that it's "handle with care"

Mother Nature can be our very best friend
So what kind of message are we trying to send

This land and its people could all disappear
The void that was left would be something to fear

The miracle of creation was God's way to say
That what he created he can take away

It's almost to late there's no time to spare
We must do our best to show that we care

Now is our time to do what we can
And tell our Lord thanks for this beautiful land

Take care of our world give it all of our love
And God will be smiling as he reigns from above

We Cannot Forget

There is a group of mostly men
Who went to a war that they could not win

There's no time to listen to what they might say
Most politicians just want them to go away

Their time in the limelight is starting to fade
Their troubles pass by them in a haunting parade

One big complaint is the PTSD
It stays on forever and won't set them free

Their story is not so unique I must agree
So where is the help that was promised to be

Is it too late for the American vet
When we need their help will people forget

Some vets will complain and speak out with pride
But will they be heard from the other side

When we stop caring for veterans of old
The country we love will start to unfold

Hear what we say while there still is some time
Or our freedom will sink and not be worth a dime

So what should we do to free us from the shame
When new vets arrive will their fate be the same

We must not give up on any of our vets
We must always remember we cannot forget

We All Need to Laugh

It's good to make fun of yourself now and then
For telling a good joke is never a sin

We all need to laugh as often as we can
It clears your mind and helps you understand

The physics of laughter is an interesting sight
It's good for your body both day and night

Laughing will help when in pain or depressed
It erases the worries and gives your body a rest

So let out a laugh and see what it can do
I'm sure you'll feel better and not have the blues

Waiting in Line

Waiting in line can be such a pain
While others move forward I still remain

How long will it take I'll be here all day
It's driving me crazy how long must I stay?

Please call my number before I go mad
Why is everyone staring at me? Do I look that bad?

I can't even remember why I got in the line
If I don't get out of here I will lose my mind

Somebody cut that's not fair to the rest
I'm tired and I am angry at the whole stinking mess

"Closed for Lunch" what's happening to me
I think I am losing it what else can it be?

I'm out of here I can't wait anymore
I will come back tomorrow but it's such a great bore

Volunteers

Volunteers are a noble career
They're givers that serve us ever so dear

Without them not much would ever get done
They work for the many and give to the one

Where would we be without them today
They're service is worthy in every way

They have a great gift they are willing to share
You become a better person whenever they're near

So reach out and give without a reward
The time is well spent and you'll never get bored

Valentine

Will you be my Valentine is a familiar request
It has lasted longer than time and endured every test

What does it mean when you're given a heart
It makes you feel special from the start

When you don't get one does it seem so unfair?
Do you start to feel lonely like there's no one who cares

Well, I want you to know that I love you so
You're always in my heart wherever I go

I hope that you feel the same way for me
Together we will live as our hearts will be free

Unlock Heaven's Door

There's one way to help you feel young
Is to live as much as you can
Don't be idle and waste all your time
Becoming like a lazy old man

When you are sick and feeling low
You don't think there's much you can do
Many have learned a lesson or two
If you want they can teach them to you

Lying around and acting tired all day
Is not a good way to go
Giving someone a helping hand
Brings new life back into your soul

Sacrifice often there's so much to gain
You can be there for others in need
When you help another without a reward
It will make you feel happy indeed

Each time you serve, the Lord smiles on you
And blessings are always in store
Giving more than you take away
Will unlock heaven's door

Truth Will Prevail

Believe all you can that truth will prevail
For no matter what happens you're not here to fail

Your life is so precious beyond what you know
And when you're confused it's hard to let go

Try not to be selfish learn how to share
For God's special gift will always be there

Help others to find their way
Always remember to pray every day

Pray in the morning pray every night
The answers you get will always be right

Trust in the Lord

The challenges of mortality never cease
You face them every day of your life
We live to find each day of peace
We're surrounded by worries and strife

We call on the Lord to rescue us
From problems we seem to find
We search for the answers to bring us peace
And to ease our troubled mind

The love of the Lord fills our soul
With a calmness we often seek
Temptations may soar beyond our control
And trap us when we become weak

Faith is the answer that sets us free
Believing when we need to know
Delight in our God will help us be
Able to achieve all our goals

We'll become stronger when we trust in the Lord
The mind and heart will unite
Our prayers will be answered to his accord
And the wrongs maybe conquered by right

To Be a Tree

The mighty tree it stands so tall
The lonely man he looks so small
I hope and pray that I could be
So tall and strong and sway so free

But I am just a lonely man
Who walks along the lonely sand
And dreams of mountains and skies so blue
With a giant forest and clear lakes so cool

He sees no war this giant green
No auto wrecks or man-made machines
Dear God, I dream and pray I will see
When all mankind is like my friend the tree

They Did Their Duty

A man goes to war and is never the same
Too much to deal with the guilt or the shame

What can a vet say to help us comprehend
There will always be wars they never will end

A Vietnam veteran is history at least
Some called them heroes others called them beasts

It wasn't a good war that made you feel right
They fought their share of battles both day and night

They did their duty to country and all
So many were changed too many had to fall

Now it's a memory so distant and far
But they have the nightmares and they have the scars

A warrior is brave in so many ways
How can we honor them each and every day

They deserve to be proud in all they have done
It's a war that was lost but the battles were won

Never forget those wounded and killed for the cause
The ones that survived deserve our applause

The Visions We Share

To be young again is a dream come true
We learn as we age that life isn't new

We get tired easier than we did before
We were always in a hurry and lived to explore

Now time is so precious we pay a high price
We dream of the days when all was so nice

The visions we share are simple today
That's because we need them that way

You're only as old as your heart wants to be
So live all you can and learn to be free

The Twelfth Man

The twelfth man is more than a teammate
He's more than a large screaming crowd
They can make a difference when the game is close
And, boy, can they really get loud

There is a spirit in a football game
That goes beyond the play
And when the fans get excited
Who knows what they might say

The players make it look easy
But we know it's really tough
Any team that plays the game
Will tell you that it gets rough

If you got the money to buy a ticket
It won't be a waste of your time
But I hope that you come ready
To stand a long time in line

Being a true fan of football
Is more than just watching the game
It's like you're on the field with them
And you share in the glory and fame

Whether they win or even if they lose
The twelfth man will always be there
To bring the team home with a loving cheer
So they can know how much that we care

The Time of Summer

Oh what a time summer can be
There's so much to do and so much to see

The air is now warmer and lifts us beyond
It's a new type of magic for the cold nights are gone

The stillness of summer surrounds the calm nights
And it shines on our shoulders as the stars seem so bright

When summer arrives our hearts start to soar
Everything is softer than the seasons before

The sunsets are sharper as they light up the sky
The stars they seem closer and are bright to the eyes

The wild fish are jumping in a deep crystal green stream
The fishers are excited much more than it seems

The sprinkle of water helps keep the grass green
The short summer nights play games with our dreams

Everything is different but in a wonderful way
It's almost impossible to discover a bad day

Only God can explain the wonders we feel
He brings us so close so our minds know it's real

We our the Stewards

We are the stewards of the world we share
And sometimes forget that it's "handle with care"

Mother Nature can be our very best friend
So what kind of message are we trying to send

This land and its people could all disappear
The void that was left would be something to fear

The miracle of creation was God's way to say
That what he created he can take away

It's almost to late there's no time to spare
We must do our best to show that we care

Now is our time to do what we can
And tell our Lord thanks for this beautiful land

Take care of our world give it all of our love
And God will be smiling as he reigns from above

The Son

The Father, the Son, and the Holy Ghost
Are the supreme beings of us all
Adam and Eve were the start of the human race
They were the very first humans to fall

The Son's mission was to redeem all mankind
To free us all from a spiritual doom
He sacrificed himself and took on our sins
Three days later he rose from the tomb

He guides and counsels us with his love
No greater love there ever could be
If we obey him and hold to the course
We will live with the Lord and be free

His life was an example of how we should live
The lessons he taught were so pure
If we could follow the path that he led
We'll make it to heaven for sure

There Was a War

If in this land
There was a war
And my son fought
Hard and was slain
Along with grief
I would share some pride
To know that he died
Not in vain

But he died in land
So far, far away
From all that he loved
And once knew
And the Lord
I do say will
Hear what I pray
And will let my poor son
Come through

It matters not
Where'ere he may be
Or how he
Was taken away
His time in my life
Was such a great gift
A treasure a memory
That will stay

There Is Always Hope

Alzheimer's is a disease of the brain
It takes you slowly for sure
There is no treatment that you can take
That anyone could call a cure

Those who suffer from this dreadful disease
Are not alone in their plight
They are surrounded by those who love them dear
And will join them as they put up a fight

There's pills to take and patches to wear
That postpone the symptoms for years
But the progression never stops moving on
Which creates such horrible fears

There's always hope that the day will come
When a cure will finally be found
That day will happen this I am sure
I just hope that I'm still around

I will put up a fight to the very end
At least as long as I can
So when it's over I've done my best
So others will begin to understand

The Power Of Love

Without a family where would I be
They are my life that sets me free

I pray for them every day and night
They give me purpose and help me feel right

Where would I go and what would I do
If I ever lost them my life would be through

They are a gift from God this I know
Each one is a treasure that makes my heart glow

To be without family is a sad sight
We need someone to love us with all of their might

Love is an action in every single way
It moves through our hearts and brings joy on the way

What can we pray for what do we need
The love of the Lord and a family indeed

The Plan

We are more than ourselves
And are truly divine
But the memory of our existence
Is gone from our mind

Being part of God's plan
Was a gift from above
The spirit he gave us
Is a sign of God's love

We came to this earth
To live and to learn
To receive a mortal body
And then to return

Our life on this earth
And all that we do
Will help us to be wiser
More loving and true

We will be tested
But we won't be alone
The Holy Spirit will guide us
Until we return home

All that God has
Can belong to us
If we can become worthy
Have faith and show trust

but great of gifts
That ever could be
is to dwell with our father
and our eternal family

The Pain Never Stops

Pain is a feeling we all have to bear
There're all kinds of pain it's hard to compare

When I'm hurting deep down inside
That's the worst kind of pain I must confide

It seems like forever the pain never stops
You're hurting so much that your heart wants to drop

You're left on your own confused and depressed
You call out for help but your mind is so stressed

Physical pain you can't often recall
Emotional pain makes your skin want to crawl

The best way to deal with pain that I feel
Is to share it with God as I bend down to kneel

He helps us to be free from all kinds of pain
It rests on his shoulders as peace we obtain

The Lord Is a Teacher

Trust in the Lord with thine heart
He has always been near from the start

If you compare all his knowledge to all that you know
His power and wisdom will lift up your soul

The Lord is a teacher there's so much to learn
Reach out to others and his respect you will earn

Listen and study to the council he'll give
It will fill you with joy each day that you live

He will show you the path you should travel each day
He is willing to listen whenever you pray

Wherever you go whatever you do
The Lord's open arms will be waiting for you

Alone you feel helpless you can't find your way
The Lord will not leave you or lead you astray

You must give him your best to show that you care
There's no need to worry he will always be there

The Journey He Made

It's painful to remember the journey he made
Or even why his memory started to fade

So much has happened can you tell me please
Why he was diagnosed with Alzheimer's disease

As sad as we were he kept his great smile
Void of all bitterness showing no guile

A new life was waiting and he got in line
Patient and eager he would never wine

All was not easy he had many bad days
But somehow was able to color the gray

His memory is now gone nothing is the same
Yet his heart is still beating with a deep burning flame

When you need courage he'll be there for you
Strong to the finish as God sees him through

The Journey

I took a look deep down inside
Far past my guilt, worries, and pride

The deeper I went the more painful it was
Will I get past the pain or discover its cause

I continued my journey exploring my thoughts
Way past the battles my mind often fought

I might understand what's bothering me
If I just go deeper I'll set myself free

Then it just happened like opening a door
So fast I was moving much deeper than before

My mind had gone the deepest it had ever been
The suffering was over the pain will now end

My spirit was free how clear I could see
A glimpse of the heavens was open to me

The sweetness of peace filled my soul
This was my quest this made me whole

The Greatest Gift of All

The love of our heavenly Father
Is the greatest gift of all
He's there when we need him
And will lift us when we fall

He hears the prayers we offer him
Especially when we pray each day
He sees the prayers that are in our hearts
And cares about all we might say

He shows us that we're not alone
Though it might be hard to believe
When we listen to his still small voice
We are blessed beyond what we can see

A blessing is a gift from God
We should always give thanks in our soul
Return the blessing by giving others a hand
Help them wherever they go

The Good Times

Most of our friends and people we know
Only see our good side that's all we will show

We have many habits both good and bad
Some make us happy some make us sad

We want to treat everyone with the best of care
In hopes that our friendships will always be there

We have lived good lives as good as can be
The places we go and the people that we see

There's so much to remember and so much to do
We look to the past and hold to the new

All the things we have done can puzzle the brain
It can give us a headache or drive us insane

The good times are there for you and for me
We must listen real softly and be ready to see

The Firefighter

There is a group of men and women who work by the bell
Some days are really quiet other days are tough as hell

They can't show fear while the fire is burning high
But when you really need them they are always nearby

Some say that their behavior may seem a little bizarre
One minute they're directing traffic the next they're cutting up a
car

They feel at ease with a tall ladder or a water-gushing hose
They can really swing an ax like nobody else knows

The truck they drive is gigantic it dwarfs any car
They handle it like a race car going near or even far

When it's really crucial when someone's life is on the line
The firefighter comes to the rescue in just the nick of time

To save a life is special but that's just what they do
Some days are really hard but every day is new

I'm thankful for their courage and their willingness to serve
We can never pay them back as much as they deserve

The Dementia Stare

Have you ever seen the dementia stare
Though they are with you it seems like no one is there

They will answer when asked and speak when there's need
But their spirit is stuck somewhere else I must concede

They're distant and quiet most of the night
And when they speak out it doesn't seem right

When you look at their face it looks far away
Then you talk to them they don't know what to say

Some say they look like they don't care at all
If you bump into them they might even fall

With all of their problems you must admit
They still show up, they're not going to quit

I'm proud of these people with the dementia stare
When you get right to it you can't help but care

The Best of Friends

There are friends that walk the extra mile
When they serve you they do it with a smile

A true friend will be there to show how they care
They will treat you wisely and always be fair

They won't ask for a reward their service is free
When the chips are down that's where they'll be

Great friends are always loyal and true
The best of friends are usually just a few

Remember having a friend is only half of the way
Being a friend makes the friendship stay

The Anguish of Pain

I have had pain through all of my life
It can cut through your soul like a surgical knife

The physical pain is hard to recall
Reliving that pain would make my skin crawl

The memory of pain has been taken from me
It's a form of God's mercy what else could it be

Emotional pain may not go away
It can haunt you forever and darken your day

It creates an agony that won't set you free
The scars that it leaves is a nightmare to see

How do you rid yourself of such anguish and pain
Only God can erase what drives you insane

So drop to your knees and plead to above
He will not forsake you he knows only love

He can help you be free of the shame you endure
You must trust in the Lord his promise is sure

I promise you that it's peace you will know
Hold on to your faith and don't ever let go

The Taste of Victory

A salesperson's work is never done
You may win the battle but the war is far from won

You set your goals then off you go
But you need to work hard to achieve those goals

When you come up short it doesn't look good
You get so disappointed like anyone would

When you taste the victory the glory is short
The next day it starts over and where is the report

It's still a great job for those who can endure
Be on the right side and when you commit be sure

The customer is right almost all of the time
And when they are wrong you walk a thin line

Be a positive person it's okay to have pride
The path may be narrow but the reward can be wide

Sunday Again

Yes it is Sunday again
And to church we all will go
For it's been a very long and hard week
And there's so much to learn and know

Yes it is Sunday again
And eagerly awaits the Lord
For us enter into his house
And pray and worship to his accord

Yes it is Sunday again
He fills our hearts as we sing
To honor our Lord Jesus Christ
Who is Creator, Redeemer, and King

Yes it is Sunday again
And the meeting has come to close
We will climb in our cars and head for our homes
With the Spirit of the Lord in our souls

Struggles

Breathing air is a simple task
Without air we could not last

Life has its struggles we all must endure
Without the challenge life would be a bore

Where would we go what would we do
We seek the trials for us to pursue

Sometimes we stumble and come up short
Alone we are doomed we must search for support

Look for the light that shines bright and clear
The path becomes steady absent of fear

Each step we take pushes us close
We conquer our struggles that test us the most

Will we ever reach the end of our trail
No it's an eternal quest that we must not fail

Rely on the Lord he will always be near
To show that he loves you and there's nothing to fear

Stretch to the End

We can't win every battle we fight
Losing happens sometimes in our life
It is what we do when we lose
How we deal with the pain and the strife

There's a part of me that says just go on
Have the faith it will all work out
The other part wants to push me down
Then I get angry and just want to shout

I must endure and not lose my dream
I must realize it's within my reach
If I just hang on a little bit longer
I will gain the wisdom that I seek

Don't throw in the towel or call it quits
When you are within reach of your goal
Hold to the rod and stretch to the end
Have faith in yourself and your soul

Stress

Someday you feel like you're ready to blow
You're so anxious you can't even think
You're all tied up in one big knot
And your spirit is beginning to sink

Some call it anxiety others say it's stress
When you're wound up so tight
Your body starts to shake all over
Your heart is pounding and nothing is right

Why does the body react in this way?
There must be some pill you can take
Is it a feeling or physical pain
You feel like your body will break

You're feeling so tense you just want to shout
You pray that it will not stay
You're hurting so much you want to cry
You'll do anything if it just goes away

You're down on your knees asking for help
You figure there's nowhere else to go
You've taken the pills you listened and talked
And finally your heart starts to slow

The nightmare is over at least for tonight
The sun shines brightly and clear
The battle subsides it was a good fight
Your soul is filled with good cheer

Still a Small Voice

You're never alone when God is near
That still small voice is there to hear

The warm feeling that comes over you
It helps you take the steps that's so hard to do

And when you step out and exercise faith
It sends God a message of power and strength

Show also courage and don't be afraid to share
With the Lord at your side there's nothing to fear

Keep moving forward all of your life
No matter the trouble no matter the strife

Give all you can to your fellow man
Do what is right and life will be grand

Step Up and Take the Lead

Don't let fear stop you from getting the help that you need
Others will follow you as you step up and take the lead

So many people want to help but they need to follow a plan
This world is filled with a lot of good who care and understand

Someone to point the direction and guide them to where they
should go
This leader should have the wisdom and be willing to learn and
know

The path they take will show courage they can do it in no other
way
To be an example to others the leader will know what to say

When crucial decisions become hard to make
A leader moves forward knowing how much is at stake

Stand for Freedom

I stand for freedom and all that is right
I'm a God-fearing man who's willing to fight

Fight for the choice to be all I can be
A life without liberty is no life for me

I wave the flag of the USA
It must keep waving is all that I pray

What kind of country will we leave to our young
Will it be weak or will it be strong

I chose to be strong in all that we do
I will go the distance for myself and for you

I'm willing to die for the right to be free
If you need a patriot you can count on me

Springtime

This is a special time of the year
Things change right before your eyes
The colors become so vivid
The clouds open up from the skies

The sun it shines more often
And the cool air starts to warm
The animals become more active
And the mountains change their form

Spring has so much to offer you
The streams are crystal clear
The melting snow feeds all of life
And brings nature also near

The grass it looks much greener
The trees they sway so free
You can hear the sounds of everything
From a waterfall to a buzzing bee

The smell of spring is amazing
There are so many smells to enjoy
Just take a deep breath and soak it all in
There's no need for you to be coy

Be thankful for what we're given
And the special time of spring
So if we listen carefully
We can hear Mother Nature sing

So Close to Your Heart

Those that we love are so close to our heart
We cling to their memories as they slowly depart

We want to do something that will keep them close by
While looking for comfort we want to know why

Why are they leaving when we want them to stay
How can we help them while they are drifting away

Hold to the good times and know how you feel
Each moment is precious and ever so real

Keep living your life the best way you know
And hold to the rod and never let go

As your day arrives and it is your time to leave
They will honor your memory and always believe

Smile

The gift of a smile can brighten our day
It raises us upward and colors the gray

A smile is the sunshine each person can show
It warms all our spirits and gives light to the soul

It requires some work when you're sporting a frown
To create a smile is much harder than it sounds

A smile will always bring you new life
It's a way to repeal all worries and strife

When you live with a smile you can truly take pride
For all those that see you will be happier inside

Sing Hallelujah

The Christmas story has been shared for over two thousand years
But every time I hear it my heart is filled with cheer

What a powerful time it must have been to witness his humble birth
The greatest event to ever take place on our entire earth

The angels sang as the star shined so bright
The shepherds witness a miracle on that cold and lonely night

And billions of spirits cried out with joy
As so much was resting on the birth of one little boy

Though Christmas has changed wherever we go
The birth of our Redeemer will ring out in our soul

So sing hallelujah as we celebrate this day
Remove the sadness from our heart especially when we pray

He is our Lord and our King the Savior to us all
Who helps us through the shadows and lifts us when we fall

Show Us the Way

Where can we go when the road looks dark
What do we do or say
Will we be lost in the deep black night
Will anyone show us the way

Sometimes life gets to hard to bear
We search for the answers unclear
When we find all that we seek
We will face it with courage not fear

Is our journey a lonely road
Will we find help from the light
It glows on the path to show us the way
It helps us to know if were right

The shadows we see may limit our hope
Beware of the mist in the air
We'll gather our course and follow the Lord
For without him we are lost in despair

Service

When you do something for someone you know
It opens a door and your spirit starts to glow

Helping a stranger is service at its best
When you're called on to serve there's no time to rest

The best way to serve is with your heart open wide
You should give all you can without showing pride

You do what you must to help them get by
Easing their pain so there's no need to cry

Call out to the Lord and ask him the way
He will show you the path you must follow each day

Take the great leap where others won't go
Trust in the Lord he'll reach into your soul

Re's-me' of the Heart

I am still here where else could I be
Life is a struggle but it's worth it to me

Some days are dark and others bring light
Sometimes I feel awkward some days I'm just right

One thing I know life is a gift
It gives us meaning and my heart a big lift

I may not be the same as I used to be
Memories fail but you can always trust in me

I may be a little rusty in some things I know
But I can learn quick and I never work slow

Sometimes I'm wrong I'm the first to admit
I won't make excuses I'll just get right to it

If I forget to show up one day
Don't send me packing I want to stay

Believe in me as I do in you
Together there is nothing we can't do

Renewal of Spirit

Is our challenge in life hard to share
Can it be more than our troubles can bear

How do we find the relief we so need
The answers aren't easy I must concede

Where do we turn to find our way
Is there no end to an awful day

I seek his soothing and healing embrace
I must find the Lord there's no time to waste

I drop to my knees and plead with my heart
I open with "My Father" before my prayer starts

I know he will hear me he always does
I thirst for his wisdom and stand strong for his cause

My burdens are lifted my joy is so real
The Lord has renewed my spirit and zeal

How free I do feel my troubles are gone
Erased by his mercy I now can move on

Reason to Hope

Do you have a reason to hope?
Or is it beyond what you can bear?
Are you staring into the darkness?
Do you feel like no one really cares?

Go back to having hope again
It will help you conquer your pains
Without it you are probably lost
The faith in yourself can't be sustained

Hope equals faith in so many ways
It gives you a chance to survive
You put on the front steps of God
It helps you feel that you're alive

Don't lose your hope keep it close by
You'll need it when times get bad
Hold yourself steady lean on the Lord
Especially when you're feeling sad

Believe in yourself you won't be let down
You didn't come to the earth to fail
Nobody said it would be easy for you
But hope will always help you prevail

Reach Out to Others

When you feel you're all on your own
Try to remember you are not alone

Though you may be lonely and feeling blue
There's always someone that cares about you

Those little sad feelings you have inside
If you're not careful they can grow to be wide

Reach out to others whenever you can
They are there to help you to understand

Don't let the darkness surround you completely
Sadness and depression can always be beat

A smile is the protection you might need
It can be ever growing like a beautiful seed

Always have a happy thought stored away
So you are prepared for a dark rainy day

Pray Me Back

I feel like I'm wandering so far away
My life is filled with so much sadness and fear
If I could change and follow the Lord every day
He can lift me and fill my spirit with cheer

Those that love me must pray me back
I will need all the help of my family and friends
For right now it is faith that I truly lack
I fear that my good days will end

I will face many giants that want control
I must find the true faith to endure
A battle will be waged for my tired little soul
I must keep my mind clean and pure

I've been told many times that I'm all on my own
There will be no one on my side
Then I feel weak and I feel all alone
I need God to surround me with his arms open wide

Through faith and prayer and trust in the Lord
His blessings will fall upon me
Peace and God's love will be my reward
Finally I'll know that I am free

I can enter the Lord's house with glory and peace
The freedom to learn all I can
I know that God's love will only increase
It's now that I truly understand

Pray to Above

Prayer is a way to speak to the Divine
It's a chance to share what's in your heart and mind

When you pray to above you show that you care
You hope for the answer and have faith it is there

Praying is not a one way road
We must carefully listen in a spiritual mode

The answers may not be what we want them to be
They will be right and they will set us free

How long and when should we pray
A prayer in your heart every moment of the day

You don't want to pray for others to see
Pray in secret and on your knees

Prayer

A prayer in your heart will help you to be strong
It frees you from worries or what might go wrong

Each time that you pray silently or on bended knee
The Lord will prepare you to be the best you can be

Prayers are a blessing to show that he cares
The Lord is close beside you he will always be there

We all want our prayers to be answered right away
Sometimes it takes longer than one night or day

But when you need him he won't let you down
He hears all our prayers he's always around

Always be thankful when you offer your prayer
Then listen real closely to what he will share

It isn't important to have your prayer be real long
A short simple prayer could never be wrong

However you pray it must come from the soul
You must pour out your heart that's when you will know

Know that he loves you in every way
For prayer is just one way to show you obey

Pets

When you get a chance
To give a pet a home
You can always say no
And find yourself alone

A pet become a friend
Loyal to all you do
They try to warm your heart
And will always count on you

It takes time and effort
And can be a lot of work
In return they will love you
And put up with all your quirks

All pets have a purpose
Their master is whom they serve
If you are lucky to have one
It's probably more than you deserve

Choose your pet wisely
Find your common ground
You will truly miss them
When they're not around

Peace of Mind

War is not the worst that we have seen
But it brings out the terror of man
It closes the door on what we call peace
And leads us on a road we don't understand

But yet we fight on
Though it may seem unfair
For those who love war
They really don't care

The Lord is our only hope
Without him we're lost
Still we must stay on course
No matter what the cost

So cling to peace live for peace
It's the only true path we find
And trust in the Lord he won't let you down
At least you will have peace of mind

Patches to Wear and Pills to Take

Smoking can become a habit
That will shorten your life for sure
As you're coughing and have shortness of breath
It becomes so hard to endure

The smoke sticks to your clothing
And gives off an unpleasant smell
Whatever you do it won't go away
You breathe like your climbing a hill

There are patches to wear and pills to take
That will help you give quitting your best
You must be determined to conquer it all
You must fight with all of your zest

You can win the battle
No matter how hard it seems
You will discover a true freedom
Beyond your wildest of dreams

The best way to stop smoking
Is to never to start at all
And if it becomes a problem
Then it's time to give us a call

We'll be there if you need us
No matter how hard it can be
To rescue you from disaster
And help you to learn and to see

Once a Marine Always a Marine

I've got a brother who was a hardcore marine
If you didn't know him you would think he's just mean

He wanted and was the best he could be
The Marine Corps way was all he could see

When he puts on his uniform it has to be right
But when fighting is needed he's ready to fight

I suggest very strongly you don't bad-mouth the corps
For when my brother is done with you you'll walk very sore

But if you need someone to be a loyal friend
My brother will be there to the very end

He's a patriot for sure in all he can do
He is not afraid to die for the Red, White, and Blue

Obedience

Obedience is a choice that God has for you
It's not always easy but it is always true

If you decide to disobey
God's special blessings can be taken away

It's not always easy to do what is right
When you do your burdens become light

When you are alone you think no one will know
God can see clearly what you try not to show

Some say it's old-fashioned to do what he commands
But you won't go astray if you follow his plan

When you're on God's team your heart will be strong
Just chart a straight course don't choose what is wrong

As you travel his road be honest and sincere
You won't be alone you have nothing to fear

His laws can be hard but you really must try
Never forget to always aim high

Nothing to Fear

Climb aboard the trip is free
Don't be afraid of what you might see
Open your eyes as wide as you can
Try to remember and to understand

Where are we going I'd like to know
Somewhere new I really hope so
You count the people who are coming along
I'll be the tour guide and sing them a song

Song of discovery a new tune I hear
We're just having fun there's nothing to fear
When do we get there I really hope soon
It's getting darker I don't see the moon

My eyes are wide open there's such a bright light
I feel so at peace it all seems so right
So many people I know everyone
I can't believe it's as bright as the sun

They are all smiling and looking at me
I've got to go further there so much to see
I feel so at home in this wonderful place
I since God is near I can feel his grace

I think this is heaven I hope that it is
There's no pain or sorrow only pure happiness
Thank you for coming with me, my good man
It makes me so happy to be together again

No Need to Cry

Some say having dementia
Is a curse of the worst kind
It may be worse than cancer
As it slowly destroys your mind

It is a horrible trick
That can haunt you every day
As for me I can deal with it
Despite what others might say

I have to make each day I live
As special as it can be
I must count my blessings every day
And look forward to all I see

When the hard days start to show
There's nothing that I can do
The ones that love me and care the most
I hope are there to see me through

I won't realize what's happening to me
I may even act like I don't care
Everything will turn upside down
And many will feel it's so unfair

At the very end will be the worst
It will be a blessing that I die
But soon I will be on the other side
And there's really no need to cry

My suffering will be over
And heaven is where I hope to go
The Lord will give his embrace
As my spirit starts to glow

The loved ones that I had lost before
Will now be at my side
And take me to a higher place
Where the light is brighter and wide

New Year Is Coming

Every year's a new year as the old becomes the past
It just becomes a memory some hope it will not last

Whatever happens the year before can influence the now
It can make your life a challenge as you try to wonder how

We must try not to live in the past if we can
It can keep us from progressing as we try to understand

Try to look to the future there is so much you can see
It's exciting to imagine what could happen to you or me

The new is filled with adventure there is so much to learn
Beyond our wildest visions life always has some turns

Where life leads you is determined by how you live
Are you mean and selfish or do you help and try to give

And then before you know it the year is coming to an end
You must start getting ready before the new year begins

Then it's time to set your goals and make sure they are right
Be sure to aim a little high but not clear out of sight

For life it keeps on going and time will never stop
Be sure to hold on tightly for what goes up will drop

Never Let Go

When you lose the one you love
It's time to turn to God above

He will lift you up when you feel low
And give you hope wherever you go

You can trust him he won't let you down
He makes life a gift so there's no need to frown

The love he shares can help you see
He will walk beside you for eternity

Call upon him whenever you can
A prayer in your heart will help you understand

You're not alone the Lord is everywhere
When you need him the most he will be there

You'll be together quicker than you know
Hand and hand you'll walk together don't ever let go

Never Leave You Alone

Every person has a challenge or two
Or maybe even more
Without our trials we cannot grow
Or be stronger inside for sure

Life is a gift and also a test
It's is more than a pass or fail
There may be hard times that come our way
It won't always be a smooth sail

Letting go of one that you love and need
May cause you to worry much more
Will they be treated with kindness and care
What trials will they have to endure

God understands the pain that you bear
He promises to be by your side
When you seek him in humble prayer
That's when it's time to confide

He will listen to all that you have to say
His compassion is greatest of all
The one that you love will not be alone
He can help your huge burdens be small

Doing the hard thing takes courage and strength
The Lord won't let you be on your own
He'll lift you up high when you need him the most
He will never leave you alone

Never Give It Up

We open our eyes in the morning
And close them usually at night
In between is a lot of living
Where our choices aren't always right

I am sure we must admit
That not everything will go well
Sometimes life turns upside down
We feel like we're trapped in a shell

It doesn't have to be constant pain
There's room for joy to finds its way
When it does you must hold on tight
Don't ever be afraid to pray

Each day is a lesson
Courage is what we learn
You must always try to step forward
Though the sign may say right turn

The light of day is joyful
While the darkness of night seems stern
How we live each moment of life
Will measure how much we learn

Never be afraid to call on the Lord
He loves you more than you know
So if you feel you're falling short
You must know that he won't let you go

So hold on tight
Show no fear
You're not alone
His love is near

Never give it up
You're not here to fail
Life is eternal
Stay close on his trail

Never

Never say can't when there's a chance that you can
Never ignore what you don't understand

Never say why when you gave it your best
Never give up when you don't pass the test

Never say who though your eyes cannot see
Never surrender when you want to be free

Never say help unless you can give
Never be lonely when it's your time to live

Never say stop when there're trials to endure
Never be scared when your mind is not sure

Never say sorry unless it comes from the heart
Never let go just hold on from the start

Never say leave me when you need them to stay
Never leave God he hears you as you pray

Never say I need you unless you're willing to share
Never go backward when the finish is near

Never say never when there's so much to learn
Never take something that you first didn't earn

Letting Go

When is it time to let them go
Will it be fast or will it be slow

One thing I know the pain will be strong
Just saying good-bye it all seems so wrong

She had a good life why should it end
The truth of it all is a new life begins

Surrounded by love ones who passed on before
She won't be alone or in pain anymore

You will go on living that's just what we do
Her memory will always be there for you

When you get tired and it's your time to go
She will join you again and your spirits will glow

Nature's Wrath

The boxes scattered around the land
Are no match for nature's wrath
The power of the mountain
Left death and destruction in its path

Nature shows no mercy
When man gets in the way
It's hard to really conquer
No matter what you say

Humanity is the victim
That pays the awful cost
When nature shows it power
Its victory is our loss

Men women and children
Disappear below the mud slide
Their cries cannot be answered
It's Mother Nature that must decide

So sad it really must be
To bury so many souls
So many are still missing
Their fate so hard to know

Nature's Battle

Spring is such a season
That everybody knows
New life is showing up everywhere
As nature puts on a show

There's thousands of flowers all over
Such a beauty to see them bloom
The fragrance fills the warming air
As the sun shines high at noon

The trees are larger than they were before
A gentle wind causes them to sway
The green of the grass starts to cover the earth
Oh what a beautiful and peaceful day

I am amazed at what I see
The color of nature so vivid and clear
As I try to gaze beyond my sight
The landscape wipes away my fears

Then I see a horrible sight
That starts to make me cry
Buildings coming from nowhere
As I watch them climb into the sky

Trees are falling everywhere
As tractors dig up the ground
Piles and piles of lifeless dirt
Are scattered all around

If nature loses
This awful war

The beauty we love
Will be no more

Pray as hard as you ever could
Make a stand for what is right
You must remember whatever you do
It is always worth the fight

There is so much at stake
We must gather all who care
It's time to make a valiant stand
What they want is so unfair

The irony of it all is so pure
For it's man who brought the plight
And yet it is so strong to see
That it's us who lead the fight

Our victory will be great
For all the human race
And God will be looking on
With such a smiling face

Nature Is Beauty

Nature is beauty in its purest form
As winter is cold and summer is warm

Nature is power when it wants to be
It can roar like a lion or buzz like a bee

There is more to nature than all that we know
It can run so strong and fast or glide so ever slow

The truth about nature is it's here for me and you
You'll never know all of its secrets no matter what you do

Nature is the freedom that passes by us every day
It serves mankind in so many wonderful ways

If you want to know nature as others have before
Immerse yourself in its magic and your heart will ever soar

When you discover nature then you'll truly understand
That nature is everything that's not made by man

Natures Resume

As the sky was turning dark blue
It was dotted with such beautiful colors
And the warm air started to cool

The trees were all mysterious
As the river ran slow
The quietness was complete
For it reached into my soul

The mountains stood high and raw
The valley was wide and green
All I could do was soak it all in
It's like nothing I have ever seen

Such beauty is a rare event
Because nature never stands still
The sun just melts into the dark sky
As I wonder if this is real

The answer to that question
Is impossible to find
What you see and feel is a miracle
That takes you far beyond your mind

Before I lay down to go to sleep
I offer a little prayer
When I wake up the very next day
That the magic of God will still be there

My Partner

I can still remember
As far back as can be
The memories that I treasure
Are the ones of you and me

We loved and laughed together
Each moment was a gift
A precious treasure away
That gave my heart a lift

Yesterdays are fading
Before today appears
When I seek the answers
I find my recent fears

All I know is nothing
Now it's all so still
Are you there to help me
My empty mind to fill

You are there to show me
I must take your hand
Time is quickly passing
Will I understand

Now you're with me always
Wherever I may go
The love that we both honor
Will fill my lonely soul

Music to My Ears

They can hear the sound of music
As it rings throughout their soul
For the tunes that play deep inside
Will follow them wherever they go

Though their memories may be weak
The joy they hear makes them strong
It opens the heart and enlightens the mind
And the spirit reveals their song

No longer the void of emptiness
Controls their feelings or thoughts
But sweet music rings within their ears
New life can now be sought

Sing out loud for all to hear
As it rings of familiar days
And let the sun shine so clear
As it warms them by its rays

Mother's Day

Everyday should be Mother's Day
We owe them oh so much
Though we are much older now
We still remember our mother's touch

Her words of encouragement
Could melt the hardest heart
And when she was disappointed in us
A tremendous guilt would start

My mother taught me everything
How to camp and how to hike
And how to catch a baseball
And even ride a bike

She showed how to live the holidays
Especially Christmas and New Year
Those memories of those special days
I treasure oh so dear

She taught me how to play fun games
And even how to fight
And when I got into a scuff
I would give it all my might

If I fell and scratched my knee
She would wipe away my tears
When I lay in bed all sick
I knew that she was near

So don't forget your mother
And the love she has for you

It's not easy to give birth
It is a painful thing to do

Every mother is not the same
No one expects them to be
They brought us into the world
Without them we could not be

Mother Nature

I looked into the sky one day
To see what Mother Nature had to say

Look at my greens look at my blues
Such pretty colors I offer you

Be still my friend don't say a word
And you will hear the chirp of a newborn bird

For I am hear to help you feel free
And soak in the sweetness as far as you see

Memories of Childhood

Children like to play and have lots of fun
They laugh and they giggle in the brightly lit sun

They like to discover things that are new
They're usually honest and talk straight to you

Alone they get nervous that's how it should be
Together with others they jump and run free

My memories of childhood were the best times of all
We could play all day with one little ball

Then when it was time to go inside
Mom would be waiting with her arms open wide

We were all very lucky we didn't need much
With hamburger helper mom had the magic touch

Now that I'm older life is so complex
You don't talk to each other now you just text

Memorial Day

Why do we celebrate Memorial Day
Once a year isn't enough I say

Our country sacrificed their very best
They rose to the occasion and took the ultimate test

What else could we ask for these heroes of old
They show courage beyond any legend that was told

Many gave so much and almost lost their lives
But the medics, nurses, and doctors helped them to survive

If you are a veteran there's so much we owe you
Your answer to us is "we do what we gotta do"

Each year I'll remember this special day of the year
And when I do I will shed a few tears

Those who died and bled for the cause
I promise their memories will never be lost

Made in the US of A

Where is America where has it been
Is it the same country we used to live in

What's made in America is always the best
American made will pass every test

Some things have turned upside down
When you look for the best it's never around

Where can we go what can we do
Everything is cheaper for me and for you

What do we stand for where do we go
Is made in China the best we can show

We better wake up before it's too late
For our children's sake we really can't wait

We must get back to made in the US of A
Or our rights and freedoms can be taken away

The True Source

Did you live the life the Lord gave you
Are you now on the real course
Have you wasted the precious time you have
Do you recognize the true source

You must pass the test you were given
If you want to go to the head of the class
You won't be graded by how many you failed
Or even how many you passed

What determines your score of today
Is the effort that you put in
To show how you honor the Lord
As you triumph over your sins

Don't get discouraged or low
Just do all that you can do
The Lord intercedes in so many ways
He's there to help you get through

So discover the life that he gave you
A brilliant life it will be
Learn to love the Lord in every way
You will know how to make yourself free

Love is Eternal

To see a young couple in love is really neat
But to witness an older couple in love now that's a treat

You may not see them hand in hand
But their hearts still touch and that is grand

The memories they share they share for life
I'm sure there were hard times with worries and strife

They had their own share of troubles that's for sure
But the lesson to learn is you must endure

The day will come when it's time to part
You can't separate what comes from the heart

Our future has hope if we just can see
That real love live forever into eternity

Live To Be Happy

Happiness is more precious than silver and gold
It helps to warm our heart when life gets so cold

It's not always easy to find the way
And try to help others get through the day

Happiness is something that all of us seek
It helps us be strong when we're feeling weak

Sharing with others is the best course
For God is the path to the only true source

Live to be happy as long as you can
How do you do it by giving others a hand

Always be glad as one can be
Your soul will be lighter and always be free

Live To Be Free

In our country we live to be free
To be whatever we want to be

We're taught to be the best that we can
That we are unique whether woman or man

If we work hard there is nothing we can't do
Discovering our dreams is what we pursue

It doesn't matter if we're strong or meek
What matters the most is the truth that we seek

The knowledge we find may be our reward
We should always remember it came from the Lord

Then get on our knees to say thank you
Believing in God is a good thing to do

Live By the Truth

Be true to yourself and let faith be your guide
Honesty is a good trait to have on your side

Telling a lie can bring you so much pain
You must live by the truth there is so much to gain

Stand for what's right in all that you do
Your life will be more peaceful in all you pursue

God will remember when you make a wise choice
He will be there to help you as you hear his still voice

Give hope to others so they can stand true
If they need help they can just lean on you

What else can you do to help find your way
Just live life sincere and you'll turn out okay

Listen While You Pray

When I am gone and you're on your own
I hope and pray you know that you're not alone

The Lord will be by your side all of the way
To comfort you bless you and listen when you pray

Your children and grandchildren will be there also
To help and strengthen you wherever you need to go

Don't worry, dear, I'll be close by
To lift you when you're saddened or you need to cry

Before you know it we'll be together again
It all will become clearer to you then

Don't be afraid I know you can be brave
God's in control for all of us will be saved

Listen To the Lord

When you listen to the Lord you must try to be still
Have faith is his words and your spirit he'll fill

The quiet peace we all long to know
Will fill our heart and refresh our souls

The calm you can feel when you worship the Lord
Is a special gift he brings with his words

The message you need is within your reach
The Lord's sacred words are given to teach

So teach with the spirit in all that you do
God's great joy will be there for you

Don't be afraid if you're worthy and bold
To give all you have as we often are told

Lift Others Up

Be an example to all that you meet
That serving the Lord will make you complete

It's not just going to church every week
You must do what you can to bless the meek

Be there for those who have no one who cares
To comfort their pain and erase all their fears

Lift others up when they're feeling low
Be humble with your gifts don't do it for show

Be a good listener as they open their hearts
Show that you care from the very start

Do all you can and ask no reward
Give all your praise and thanks to the Lord

Life Isn't Over When Your Going to Die

Life isn't over when you're going to die
It may seem unfair as life passes by

We must keep on going what else can we do
If you lose hope your dreams will go too

Sometimes the pain is to much to bear
You feel all alone does anyone care

Well let me tell you that isn't true
The Lord's close by to be there for you

Perhaps you have forgotten how to pray
Have you been on yours knees at least once a day

Call out his name he loves you so much
He can heal your spirit with one simple touch

Live your last days as much as you can
Have faith in the Lord and his heavenly plan

Life is a gift we never should waste
With all kinds of flavors for us to taste

Avoid the bitter look for the sweet
Savor each day for each day's a treat

Life is a Adventure

The new year is coming
The old year is gone
It's time for the future
And time to move on

Life is an adventure
There is so much to do
We can't do it all
In one year or two

That's why we have
A whole life to live
We must try to share
It's our turn to give

Don't be afraid
When it's your time to go
The Lord will be waiting
He will always love you so

With his arms open wide
And bearing a warm smile
He will remove are your bitterness
And erase all your guile

Life Is a Journey

I want to lift everyone that I can
To look to the future and think life is grand

To rid themselves of the pain of before
To find the strength that helps them to feel sure

Sure of the hope of a bright sunny day
That good will happen as you move on your way

Life is a journey we all must endure
And hope we can live a life that is pure

Enjoy the gift that a good life can bring
Always give thanks to the Lord our great king

When life comes to an end you can say with great pride
I tried to live my life on the right side

Life is a Gift

When you're fighting a fatal disease
Your spirit can become very worn
Nothing seems to lift you out of the dark
You wish you were never born

There is an answer to all you feel
Your soul just needs a lift
So when you pray very hard
The Lord will provide you a gift

What could this be in such a hard time
How can I ever feel good
Give me a clue of what I must do
What have I misunderstood

Life is a gift as long as we live
We all share the beautiful earth
We are never alone we're so close to home
He's been with us way before birth

When you feel God's love inside
Your life is complete once again
Be at peace with all that you do
The truth is life never ends

It's just a change of address
There's still much more to see
Your old tired body is taking a rest
So the spirit can soar and be free

Life Goes On

As the world turns life goes on
We keep on going till our troubles are gone

What can we do when the future becomes the past
Where would we go how long would we last

Who's there to help us besides our true friends
They will always be there to the very end

So many things occurring each day
They come and they go in their own special way

Don't be in a hurry it matters not who you are
Just take it all in and shine like a star

There's nothing to fear it's all there to see
You should not worry you were born to be free

Always live life the best that you can
And always be willing to give a helping hand

Life is a Special Gift

Life is a special gift
That brings us joy and peace
But sometimes things aren't so good
That's when pain and suffering increase

It's how we really live our life
That determines which way we sail
Doing our best is the final test
A test we must never fail

Surviving all the storms of life
Must be are truest quest
The effort that we all put forth
Has to always be are best

Be not afraid but face your fears
For God will help you win
The victories that you have in life
Truly has no end

Let the Wind be on Your Side

Why can't I remember like other people do
Where is my mind going and how long will it take
Will the good days be hard to find
I'll sleep all day and I'll never awake

I used to forget once in awhile
Now it's a constant concern
I'm good at saying how sorry I am
My challenge is trying to learn

I understand others and how thy feel
How can I explain the emptiness inside
Sometimes I feel like crying out loud
Most of the time I just want to hide

They say it's a disease that can't be cured
No matter how much money you spend
Confused by the symptoms as the day goes by
It blows you off course with a strong wind

It all looks so sad in a dark lonely way
The depression can control what you do
If you let all the worry define who you are
Then your troubles will never be through

Say loud and clear I'm not going to lose
Show that you mean what you say
Let the wind be on your side
And blow all the sorrow away

Know What's Real

Memories are forgotten
To much goes on inside
The mind is always searching
My thoughts could never hide

I want to be alone now
How lonely do I feel
I long to find my freedom
I need to know what's real

Take my hand and guide me
Help me seek the way
I am not afraid now
As long as you will stay

I have no secrets to share
My life's an open book
The path I travel is so narrow
Come and take another look

Knowledge Is Freedom

Be smart and wise as you live out your days
A quick mind will be helpful in many ways

Learn all you can don't run away from school
A good education makes you nobody's fool

Read all you can and learn to love books
It's okay to be smart don't care how it looks

Train yourself how to become wise
Knowledge is freedom and that is no lie

Share with others all that you've learned
They will help you succeed when it is your turn

Try to remember there are people smarter than you
Not everything you learn will be easy to do

Nature Is a Gift

Nature is a gift from God's great hand
It's the purest form of living that we can understand
He puts it close within our reach so we enjoy its awe.
Its grandeur and its majesty both large and even small

What a responsibility we have to treat this gift with care
Be thankful for all we see show respect for all that's there

Don't abuse what God has made keep it clean and pure
Be aware of all we do or this treasure will disappear

Only man can cause its fall it's more fragile than you think
A little change can help its rise or quickly start to sink

Gaze in wonder for all you can see
Give God your thanks and be the best you can be

Live Life Large

Live your life the best you can
Find adventure wherever you go
Don't get upset if you don't understand
That life is not a movie or TV show

Being alive is a precious gift
Live life large is what you must do
Every step you take will give you a lift
Avoid the false and seek only the true

When you discover where you need to be
You won't be controlled by your fears
You're just in a place where you can be free
A place where the Lord is near

Be true to yourself when it's time to decide
The path that you follow each day
There is no harm in showing pride
Don't let anyone take that away

When it's all said and done and the day turns to night
Be thankful when you kneel down to pray
Trust in the Lord with all of your might
Listen closely to all he will say

Letting Go

When is it time to let them go
Will it be fast or will it be slow

One thing I know the pain will be strong
Just saying good-bye it all seems so wrong

She had a good life why should it end
The truth of it all is a new life begins

Surrounded by love ones who passed on before
She won't be alone or in pain anymore

You will go on living that's just what we do
Her memory will always be there for you

When you get tired and it's your time to go
She will join you again and your spirits will glow

Keep Us Safe

The old veteran walked though the door
He didn't move as fast as he used to before

He still has a gleam that shines in his eyes
But he carries the memory of the brothers who died

So much sacrifice that he had to bear
Some on his own some he could share

We cannot forget what the vets have done
The war that we lost and the wars that we won

They may look older than most of us
But they stepped up to serve and deserve our trust

We enjoy the freedom that they fought for
When it got rough they were ready for more

All they need is our thanks and respect
For keeping us safe and our enemies at check

Joy Is Always There

Don't look for what you can't do look for what you can
Be a positive person and help others to understand

If you look for the bad in all that you do
Your chances for a happy life might as well be through

Try to smile whenever you can and even when you're sad
Avoid anger always and steer clear of being mad

Look for the joy it's always there
It follows those who show they care

Be an example of a loving soul
That radiates gladness wherever they go

Some will be critical some just won't care
Don't let that stop you from wanting to share

Love is a powerful path to be on
You will always be needed when others are gone

Joy In the Journey

Life puts us on many trails
The trek may lead us to amazing sights
Or maybe will travel to a real dark place
Where the sun doesn't shine and it's always night

The hardest part is to stay on course
The path we travail may be narrow and long
How can we make it what will we do
Each step that we take could be right or wrong

We must find joy in the journey
Because life is a gift
When we find ourselves sad
Our heart will need a lift

God will always be there
Keep our eye on the prize
He wants to help us
He is loving and wise

The spirit that we're given
Can be our best friend
We must hold to the rod
It will guide us to the end

It's a New Year

A new year is finally on its way
What's not here tomorrow is yesterday

Predicting the future is a difficult plan
The world is really hard to understand

What becomes current will fade into the past
The world seems to be moving too fast

We must always keep thinking of how to survive
And learn real quickly how to stay alive

Don't show your fear whatever you do
Remember what will happen is all up to you

Time will move forward that is a fact
If you want to keep up you must know how to act

Look where you're going stay on the course
Don't wander away you might lose your source

Is There More to Thanksgiving

How many times do we say thank you? Not enough I fear
It seems not important though we celebrate it each year

Gratitude is a special way to show others that we care
To honor our great friendships and learn to always share

Is there more to Thanksgiving Day than the turkey that we eat
Can we do something special to make the day complete

Show the people that we love how thankful we can be
Open our heart to everyone so all of us could see

Be sure to thank the Lord above for this awesome day
Without his help we would all be lost and never find our way

Thanksgiving has two meanings I hope we understand
We must give and learn to be thankful for the bounties of our land

Each night we should be praying to God who stands above
Then thank him for his kindness and the outpouring of his love

I Served My Country Well

I served my country well
I did my time in hell
I fought the battle we all did lose
Without the drugs without the booze

Why did we die why did we bleed
Was it for power or was it for greed
And now our country wants to forget
The sacrifice of the Vietnam vet

Someday war will come again
What could we tell our sons
What honor could we promise them
When they see what we have done

How sad and lonely they will feel
As they march off to war
With stories of the older vets
Who fought in vain before

So now I tell America
From me and all my friends
Who gave their arms legs and lives
So freedom would never end

I Need to Be Free

You're traveling on a peculiar trail
Each step you take something new is unveiled

Then you come up against a great wall
The first thing you notice is the wall is too tall

You look to the left and then to the right
It keeps on going far out of sight

How will you get on the other side
That is a puzzle you must confide

If only the wall had a way to get through
You could continue your trek and all that is new

Suddenly you discover a transparent door
It is very strange that you had never seen it before

The trail keeps on moving on and on
Far past the door the wall and beyond

The path still gets better beyond what you see
But the door is locked and you don't have the key

Then you realize what's in store for you
You can no longer move forward no matter what you do

You call out to the Lord "I need to be free"
Please help me, God, I must find the key

Then the door opens all on its own
Your eyes stop crying and your heart ceases to moan

The trail is now clear for you to move on
Now all your worries and troubles are gone

You have discovered what eternity truly can be
It's never ending you will for ever be free

I'm Haunted With Guilt

How can I tell you how bad I feel
You were so young and so was I
The pain of that day has lasted forty-five years
My journey was to go home yours was to die

Can you forgive me I've asked many times
How short a life span can be
If I could take back what I did to you
I would starve for the chance to be free

What kind of family did you leave behind
How could I have eased their pain
Why can't I just go ahead and move on
Is it your ghost that still remains

I'm haunted with guilt for what I have done
No matter what anyone could say
I call out to the Lord high above
Forgive me, dear God, I must pray

I long for the chance to see you again
And tell you how wrong I had been
When that times comes I will let out a shout
Now that's when the real healing begins

If I could repent and be freed of my sin
What a wonderful day that would be
The Lord could release me of this horrible wrong
I would have joy for all of eternity

I Love the Beach

The beach is a beautiful and magical place
It warms the soul and tans the face

It can be so exciting but in a peaceful way
When you're there you'll want to thank the Lord each day

The sand has a sparkle that warms your feet
The crisp ocean air you breathe in can smell so sweet

The waves how they beat against the never-ending shore
It enlightens your spirit as you search and explore

There's so much life in the forever-blue sea
It's magic and wonders expose what is free

You must listen intently as the waves never cease
Their soothing sound brings you comfort and peace

You may want to stay there forever as some people do
For nowhere in the world is nature so true

I'll Never Regret

I'll never regret the day we first met
I hope that you feel the same
You're the only one that I truly loved
I'm glad you carry my last name

We were very young and leaned on each other
To get through the troublesome days
Two individuals traveling the same path
We held together in so many ways

We are getting a little bit older now
And wiser in our advancing years
So when things get tougher on us
We are not swallowed up by our fears

Stay by my side as long as you can
How quickly the future passes by
Together there is nothing we can't do
As long as we give it a try

I Know He is Free

He wants to fight with all that he commands
But he's losing the battle and doesn't understand

Oh how I wish I could bear his pain
Shield him from suffering erase all his shame

Now I am helpless what can I do
I will hold him closely until he's through

I know where he is going and soon he'll be there
The Lord will be close to show how he cares

Now I will miss him but I know that he's free
His worries are now over now what happens to me

I must go on now that he is gone
Someday it will be my turn to move on

When we unite I will joyfully sing
Surrounded by angels with such beautiful wings

Then we will share a wonderful peace
The joy that follows will never cease

I Got Swallowed by Horny toad

I got swallowed by a horny toad
When I was just a lad
Now let me tell you, fellas
I'm feeling kind of bad

Three long years had passed me by
Before he coughed me up
My girl was wed my dog was dead
I lost my coffee cup

Now the moral of this story
Is as plain as you can see
If you get swallowed by a horny toad
I'll bet you think of me

Hope is Near

Don't give in whatever you do
Hope will always be there for you

If your challenges seem hard to bear
Remember that the Lord always will care

Hope can be a way of life
It battles the anger and conquers the strife

So when you are struggling you need not to fear
For where there is hope the Lord will be near

Believe and trust in all that is true
You won't be alone no matter what you do

Give hope a chance it never will fail
And hold your ground for good will prevail

Hope

There is nothing the body can't bear
When hope is there to show you care

Traveling through life can be a slippery slope
Especially when you have lost all of your hope

Giving hope for those in need
Is truly a noble and honorable deed

With hope on your side you really can't lose
Things will go right as you learn how to choose

We travel a path that becomes empty and dark
It swallows you up like a man-eating shark

You feel there's no hope you're lost and confused
This is ever so true when someone has been abused

What can hope do to brighten your day
When all seems lost it's time to pray

Hope equals faith and faith makes you whole
It tears down the darkness and brightens your soul

When God intervenes you surely won't fail
The truth makes it clear and hope will prevail

Hold to Your Faith

Faith is something we all must have
To make it through our daily life
Without it we would be lost for sure
Surrounded by all our worries and strife

It gives us strength to push along
It helps us find our way
When we're confused and really lost
Faith will always save the day

Faith is belief in something unseen
It's believing when there's nothing there
You must trust in the Lord in all that you do
And know that he always will care

We are sent to this earth to learn all that we can
It's not easy it wasn't meant to be
The more you try to understand
The clearer that you will see

Hold to your faith trust in its power
The Lord will always be there for you
You are never alone or on your own
When you need him he will know what to do

Hold On

If you're the one who gives the care
Your challenge is strong and may seem unfair

You must endure what comes your way
And hold your ground as they're slipping away

Be there to listen as long as it takes
Be able to give though your heart wants to break

Cherish the time with those that you love
Hold to the memories and pray to above

Be strong if you can life will go on
Don't lose your hope when your loved one is gone

He Will Set You Free

Dementia is a very serious disorder
It attacks the brain and has no borders

Your memory leaves and nothing remains
All you're left with is a dying brain

It just isn't fair how it picks who will die
If you're wealthy or smart it won't pass you by

The older you get the higher the chance
What can you do now you must take a stance

Wherever you go whatever you do
Trust in the Lord he will be there for you

You can get through this you can put up a fight
Laying down and giving up just isn't right

Keep the door open do all that you can
Life is worth living you just need a plan

Plan for the future be all you can be
Show faith in the Lord and he will set you free

He's Now In Heaven

I miss my dad he's been gone for a while
He always knew how to make me smile

On Friday we would often play cards
He was always willing to help in the yard

He said he was lonely since Mom was gone
His house was so quiet there was always a TV left on

He often spoke loud because he couldn't hear
He was blind in one eye but he never showed fear

He fought in two wars a sailor was he
When I got my medal he was so proud of me

He's now in heaven with Mom at his side
Just waiting for the rest of us with arms open wide

Heroes

Where do heroes come from
What makes them so unique
Every hero has a purpose
They bring courage to the weak

What makes heroes so special
It's the service that they give
They are there when you need them
They show us the right way to live

They are there to lift us from the shadows
And bring us into the light
They are not afraid to show you
That life is worth the fight

So when you're down and lonely
And you feel like you might fall
A hero comes to the rescue
And is willing to give their all

A hero can be anyone
That goes the extra mile
Their brave and kind in all they do
And they do it with a smile

He Is Our Hero

The comic book may tell us what a real hero should be
But in real life things are different for you and for me

A hero can be a survivor who won't call it quits
He just wouldn't give up that's a hero I must admit

We all have a hero should all heroes act the same
Is there one special power or one super name

If you think hard enough you'll know that can't be true
Every hero has a purpose and a mission they must do

There is one hero that's the greatest of them all
That's our Lord and Savior who lifts us when we fall

We can talk to him so clearly when we pray on bended knee
If we are sincere in all we do and say the Lord will set us free

A Hard Wooden Floor

Once I went to the old country store
I wasn't doing much my life was a bore

I met an old man I had never seen before
He was dancing the jig on the hard wooden floor

I asked him his name as he continued to dance
He stared right at me as if in a trance

I asked him again as I let out a yelp
I looked at the others who offered no help

And finally he spoke just one single word
He answered "why" how strange and absurd

I had enough from this coy little guy
I hollered so loud I let out a cry

What is your name I won't ask you again
He calmly answered me back "why" as he continued to grin

That's all I could take I now had enough
Now he will see that I can be tough

I hit him right square then I hit him once more
But I swear he was still grinning as he fell to the floor

Now it was just him and on that hard wooden floor
Until a little old lady walked through the door

She looked at me with pain in her eyes
And let out a scream "why o why"

What could I say I just lost my cool
The answer was senseless I felt like a fool

Then the old man stood up and still had his grin
But I had given him a bloody nose and cut on his chin

She came over to comfort him and started to cry
Again she cried out "why o why"
At that moment I realized what I had done
I beat up an old man that was just having fun

What is his name I asked as she carried him by
His name was Wyatt but we just call him why

I am not having fun my life still a bore
As I'm setting in jail on a hard wooden floor

Hard to Repent

Sometimes we fail to think
We just do whatever we choose
We don't worry about what it means
Or even the important things we might lose

But time has a way to bite you back
And the pain lingers for a while
We want the hurt to go away
No one is laughing there's no reason to smile

We drop to our knees and plead with remorse
It haunts us ever so long
Can we be forgiven for what we have done
Why would we ever do something so wrong

I can't take it back the scar will not heal
The hurt will sting for a long time
I'm deep in a canyon it is long and high
There is no way out unless I climb

Such a simple mistake I wish I could hide
But all I can do is accept the blame
I must admit my guilt and plead to the Lord
Only he can forgive my mistake and erase my shame

Halloween

There is so many holidays
We celebrate each year
But there's one special night
That brings children excitement and cheer

It's become very commercial
That's a fact to be seen
Many love to celebrate
The time of Halloween

The stores get excited
As the night starts to get close
There's costumes to buy
Like witches and ghost

Then there's the candy
That kids love to eat
It's not good for their teeth
But to them it's a treat

That night when they go out
With their bags in their hands
They will try to fill them
With as much as they can

All will stand at the door
To see who they will meet
When the door opens up
They will shout out "trick or treat"

The houses are decorated
To scare the old and the young
And the parties are everywhere
They provide lots of fun

Some say they love Halloween
More than any other holiday
To me that is scary
That's all I can say

When October is over
Halloween has passed by
You'll have a year to recover
Be ready because time can sure fly

Grandchildren Are a Joy

To write a poem for a grandchild
Is a special treat for me
It allows me to get closer to them
So the reader can truly see

I have nine grandchildren
And everyone is a prize
I hope you will know them better
As you see them through my eyes

I will start with oldest
And end with the youngest of them all
Each is so special to me
Though they range from small to tall

Josh is now a man
Still young this is true
But they don't get any purer
He's kind and giving to

Hannah is such a beauty
It's obvious that she cares
She's gentle but sincere
What she has she tries to share

Lettie is a rare gift
Filled with talent beyond her age
To watch her draw is amazing
Her life will make a wonderful page

Isaac is a go getter
It's obvious he'll be a success
He's not afraid to do the work
And will give it his very best

Katherine is a special jewel
She has charm that will win
Though she may be shy sometimes
She is willing to jump right in

Reagan is a rare beauty
As fearless as one could be
To watch her when she dances
Is a wonder for all to see

Ireland is the strong one
And is not afraid of much
She climbs through life with eagerness
And she has a magic touch

Paisley is a charmer
But she does it with great style
She's a little girl of sweetness
She will rule you with her smile

Silver may be the youngest
But it's easy for all to see
She will go far in her life
Oh how she loves to be free

I tried to catch their spirits
In such a special way

But how do you describe perfection
I just love them is all I can say

Good Days

If you do this your troubles won't mount

Each day passes by some good and some bad
We enjoy to be happy and don't want to be sad

Every day is a new day that's how it should be
If you look for the bright side clearly you'll see

When those bad days come rolling around
Try to be happy don't let yourself get down

A good day is worth all the effort you do
Remember the Lord will be there for you

He knows how to turn the bad into good
So it's time to cheer up live life like you should

God Only Knows

When life is lost there's a special cost
Where money can never go
Each person gone still lives on
Inside of another's soul

The pain is real and can't heal
No matter what someone does
They strain there eyes and often cry
When they're thinking of who it was

Remember this you'll always miss
The memory of one you loved
But in your mind you will find
God's peace that comes from above

So where we go God only knows
It's strictly a matter of choice
The closer we get we have to admit
Its time for us to rejoice

God Loves Us All

God loves us all more than we know
His spirit is with us wherever we go

We can't see God in his perfect form
When he is near we always feel warm

He teaches so gently to love all we can
To do what is right and follow his plan

It won't always be easy a challenge we'll face
He'll be there to help us and fill us with grace

He has given us a tool to help us be free
When we need him we should fall to our knees

The answer will come when it's the right time
He will shower us with blessings we know are sublime

Give Love a Chance

Love is more than a feeling
It's more than a way of life
There's more to it than just being married
To a husband or even your wife

Love has a special message
Sent to us from God above
We really don't understand
Until we feel God's love

God's love is eternal
It will never leave our soul
No matter what we do in life
Or even wherever we go

We may not feel God's love
Especially with a hardened heart
We must open up and let him in
We don't need to be savvy or smart

When true love does become a feeling
It will burn deep down inside
It warms your body and soul
Your feelings have nothing to hide

Always give love a chance
God's love won't let you down
Wherever you are he'll be close
He can make a smile from a frown

God's love never leaves you
It surrounds your spirit with peace
He will be there to lift you
His love will never cease

Friends

True friends are here to stay
They give much more than they take away

They know how to listen when you need them to
Their words are wise and usually true

They won't leave you when the chips are down
When the road is rocky they will still be around

Real close friendships will last for a life
You are very lucky if they are your husband or wife

If you lose a friend the pain is deep and long
When you gain friend you feel happy and strong

A friendship is a two-way street
To be a friend makes the circle complete

Free from Pain

Abuse is a word we all learn to hate
Its sting can leave your soul in an awful state

All that hurt may make you want to hide
It steals your respect and erodes all your pride

How can we move on and deal with the pain
The scars can be real and so can the shame

The memories are strong though your mind wants to be free
You can close your eyes tight but still you can see

Who can help you what can they do
Let God have your pain he will take it from you

Pray to be free have faith that you can
The Lord has suffered all he truly understands

With Gods help your mind can become clean
You may become weak but on God you can lean

The past can be gone the good future is near
No longer the pain no longer the fear

Oh what a blessing to finally be free
Now you can follow your true destiny

Freedom Is a Privilege

Freedom is a privilege
That we can all enjoy
If we live our lives the best we can
We must never try to annoy

Many have gone before us
And blazed a path to be free
Now it's our time to Annie up
Stop thinking what's in it for me

What we want and what we get
May seldom be the same
As for me I have made mistakes
But there's nobody else to blame

I will pay my dues
And even the score
As I try to emulate
The heroes of before

Even though I must keep the faith
Sometimes I might start to fall
I must keep going and always believe
That it's my turn to stand up tall

Freedom

Where I go I need to be
Longing for truth to set me free

I strive for freedom in all I do
I hope that my strength will get me through

But if I become weak in any way
May someone lift me up is all I can pray

I'm willing to die for the country I love
I know God will watch over me from above

Is there a lesson I need to learn
I seek your trust which I am willing to earn

Together we show that freedom will reign
As we unite we form an unbreakable chain

It can last a lifetime wherever we go
To be a shining example to all that we know

Forgivness

Forgiveness is a powerful word
To define it is so hard to do
So what it might mean to others
Could be different than what it means to you

Why is it so hard to forgive one another
When we really should give our best
Forgiving ourselves becomes the hardest
It's more of a challenge than the rest

We seem to be burdened with so much guilt
It pulls us down so very deep
And when we try to pull ourselves up
The path that we follow is too steep

When we learn to forgive ourselves
That's when we feel truly free
The burden that we carry deep inside
Is all that we seem to see

Forgive yourself and do it now
Don't put it off another day
Free yourself from your heavy burdens
Seek the Lord as you kneel to pray

Flag of the USA

The flag is special symbol
It represents a country when it waves
Most countries are proud of their flag
It's an emblem of sacrifice of the brave

There are patriots who gave their lives
So their flag can stand tall and sway free
These are heroes we should never forget
Their courage will live on in our history

Some say a flag is just a piece of cloth
That waves in the wind all day
I disagree with all of my heart
Just try taking my flag away

I'm very proud of the flag of the USA
I will wave it as much as I can
And to all who disgrace our American flag
There is something you don't understand

You disgrace an American way of life
I guess I feel real sorry for you
For what you dishonor is a symbol of right
Hooray! For the red, white, and blue

Fitness

Being healthy is the right thing to do
It lengthens your lifespan to a decade or two

Staying healthy is a lot of work
Don't take it lightly but don't go berserk

Exercise often and eat the right foods
Be a positive thinker maintain the right mood

Don't throw in the towel when you're feeling low
That is the time when you can't let go

Strive to be fit work at it each day
It will all be worth it you must not delay

Always remember take care of your health
The value is priceless far greater than wealth

Feel All Alone

I get so confused I can hardly breathe
Sometimes I feel all alone
All of the help I'm supposed to have
Just jumped ship and I'm on my own

Where can I go when I feel that I'm lost
How can I get the help that I need
Everyone has an answer for me
What chance do I have to succeed

I have to learn what's best for me
Why is it so hard to understand
It should be clear and easy to solve
Why won't somebody show me the plan

Who do I trust where can I go
I know the Lord won't let me down
I just have to get on my knees and pray
Then listen so softly for his sound

Then I can see that I'm never alone
He's walking right beside me
His arms are open wide and strong
Now I know I will always be free

Family

Family is a special word
It seems easy to define
When you take it all apart
It can baffle the brightest mind

There are all kinds of families
Some carry the same last name
In nature it's the mystery
Why all life seems the same

A family has a history
That can take you back so far
It can answer so many questions
Of where you came from and who you are

A family can bring you great strength
Because they really care
When you feel alone and lost
Their love is always there

Family is the center
Of God's wonderful plan
He can solve all the mysteries
That seems so hard to understand

We are born into a family
That surrounds us with much love
And if we really need it
We can call on God above

Not every family is perfect
Sometimes they bring you pain
But if you try to love them
Your efforts won't be in vain

Families can cross lives borders
They can join you on the other side
So when you leave this world
They're waiting with arms open wide

A family is one of the greatest gifts
That God can give to us all
It brings us into his presence
And saves us from the fall

Faith, a True Course

Faith is such a special word
It rings with strength and peace
And gives to each one of us
A hope that will not cease

Sometimes life seems all so dark
The road is marred with haze
It passes by us ever so quick
And leave us in a daze

But faith makes our path crystal clear
Our journey is straight and true
It opens the doors that are usually closed
And the old and forgotten become new

Believing is a way of life
No one can mar the course
For truth will prevail and always win
When the Lord becomes our source

Faith And Beyond

Faith is the anchor for the soul
It follows us wherever we go

Losing a loved one is an awful plight
But when faith comes along things turn out all right

God has a way of steering you straight
He mends what you have lost and carries your weight

Things aren't the same I guess that's okay
For God is in control and will show us the way

The ones that we love who are gone from our sight
Someday will return to bring us new light

Eyes of the Lord

It's not the fall that causes the pain
It's being afraid to get up again

Some people feel that to fail is to lose
But giving up is the worst step to choose

No one's a failure in the eyes of the Lord
Keeping the faith brings the greatest reward

Seek out his help for the things that are tough
With the Lord on your side nothing's too rough

Remember to thank him when the job is done
For he knows your challenge more than anyone

Easter

Each year we celebrate in a special way
When the Lord rose from the dead on Easter day

For some it's a fun day filled with cheer
And the money that's spent helps business each year

We must try to remember what happened that day
And worship our Lord in every way

Death is denied its awful sting
For all will rise to shout and sing

Glory to our Lord our Redeemer and King
For resurrection brings immortality to everything

Life becomes new no one's a slave
We will live again as we rise from the grave

The Lord will reign with power and glory
He will show us all mercy as we share our story

Judgment will come as he reigns from above
A kind and dear Savior that knows only love

Each Step We Take

Traveling down the lonely road
May seem like no one cares
When someone helps you carry the load
The trip is light to bear

Each step we take if on our own
The journey appears undone
There is no need to cry or moan
Together you are more than one

Do not fret if another is near
To lend you a helping hand
Be thankful for the one so dear
Who will truly understand

No matter where you go or where you have been
Our Lord is always there
To help you have the strength within
Your burdens he will share

Donuts

Everyone loves something sweet
And donuts are my favorite to eat

Not every donut has a hole in the middle
Some are filled with a lot or a little

A cop loves donuts I don't know why
Maybe because they're smaller than a hot apple pie

Donuts are not so healthy to consume
If you ate only donuts your belly would balloon

Think twice each time you take a bite
If you eat all of the donuts you might start a fight

I love donuts is the last thing I'll say
My heart will break if you take them away

Don't Lose Hope

Down and out is story of many
To many I must say for today
What can we do to help with this plight
It will only get worse in every way

Unemployment figures are way too high
Jobs are not easy to find
Finding a good job is like winning the lottery
The world is in need of a sign

How can we turn our economy around
What miracle do we have to do
People are struggling in so many ways
Bankruptcy can only help a few

Don't lose hope we're not here to fail
We got ourselves into this mess
If we work hard we can find a way
It will not be easy I confess

Take a step forward we can't fall behind
Together we know we can win
We have to acquire the right frame of mind
We must fight for our rights to the end

Dementia

Things aren't like they used to be
This causes stress and depression in me

I can't remember the way I could
This makes it harder to be understood

Sometimes I see things I know are not there
Or my mind tells me I'm being treated unfair

Then I start shaking for no reason at all
If I stand up I get dizzy afraid I might fall

My wife says I act out my dreams while I'm asleep
The whole situation can make a man weep

There is no cure for the symptoms I show
They will only get worse now that's hard to know

I still must keep going they might find a cure
For now all I can do is try to endure

Demented

When will it darken
Either day or night
My eyes are wide open
Where is my sight

How can I touch you
If I don't know the way
Why did you leave me
You promised to stay

Who do I hear now
Where do I go
Was I just there
Does anyone know

I have a question
The answers are not there
Does anyone hear me
Are there people who care

The light is still fading
I will lose what is mine
No one to help me
My soul can not shine

Death and Beyond

Death comes to us in many ways
In many shapes and forms
Some say death can be very cold
Others say that it is warm

In reality it's a change of address
A time for our soul to be free
The body will rest for a while
But soon they will unite for eternity

Death is not final but it is all inclusive
Everyone will experience this event
It takes us all in our due time
No one will be able to stop or prevent

But that's okay it's not that bad
Unless we surround it with fear
Though your love one may seem far away
In truth they are ever so near

No one in their right mind wants to die
They would deny it as long as they can
So when the time comes the Lord is in control
He will be there to take your hand

Together you'll walk through the Vail
The light will be as bright as the sun
You will be encircled by family and friends
You will know and love everyone

You won't be idle during this amazing time
There is so much work to be done

But you won't get tired like you did before
You'll feel great as you bless everyone

Darkness

Sometimes life can get very dark
It prays on you like a man-eating shark
Your mind goes blank it's called a stupor of thought
And when you wake up your brain is all shot
Add a cup of depression and you got yourself in a mess
This happens to me often I have to confess
Nothing seems clear you're dumped into a maze
You struggle to exit but everything is a haze
Where is my clarity why am I so lost
I have to do something no matter the cost
Maybe I can meditate and hope I can get out
I am so tied up that I just want to shout
Where is the peace where can I go
There must be a place were calmness will flow
Sometimes my writing helps me endure
The shadows brighten and I feel all so sure
A deep breath or two will show me the way
I'm glad that it's over the night has turned to day

Creation

Mother Nature is our best friend
She always around and will never end

All of the animals have their own place
Plant life surrounds us and fills its own space

Creation is a gift that shines from above
The beauty is amazing as he shows his great love

The earth sun and stars have no end
I can see forever where does it begin

I witness eternity as I look up in the night
For life continues even beyond my sight

God is the maker of all that we see
He is our Creator and set us all free

Columbus

Columbus was just a man
Like any other man could be
He had dreams of awesome wonder
And a strong desire to be free

He was a tremendous sailor
And could face his fear straight on
Where he traveled he always knew
That there must be more beyond

Think of the courage he had to have
To travel beyond what we know
He overcame his fear and doubts
He would not let his dream go

All that he discovered
And all the wonders that he found
He was a man of courage and mystery
Who proved the world was round

Now look at how we travel
Across the world in a day
Beyond the world that we call home
And nothing will get in our way

Cold As Ice

The wind is blowing
The air is cold
It chills my body
Right to my soul

How can I warm
The inside of me
A roaring new fire
Or a pot of hot tea

Though I am freezing
Right to the bone
I'm sure to find
That I'm not on my own

The love from a friend
Can warm me inside
There is no need to fear
And nothing to hide

So though my body
Maybe cold as the ice
The warmth from my heart
Will make everything nice

Christmas to Treasure

I think of the Christmases I had before
I cherish the memories my heart wants to store

When I was young I was filled with dreams
The magic of Christmas would make my eyes gleam

When Christmas comes I glow with zeal
There is a special joy that we all feel

I treasure the love that this day brings
And look forward to the songs we sing

The deep warm feelings of the pure white snow
Will travel with me wherever I go

Christmastime is a great time of year
The children are happy that Santa is near

Have a great time as you deck the halls
And try to be cheerful and kind to all

Christmas Memory

Many years have passed me by
Christmas has shared them all
This joyous season a special time
Of fond memories I still recall

The faces, the names, the places I have been
All lost in my quick growing past
But a gentle reminder of Christmas before
Renews a great joy that will last

Sparkle, glitter, toys, and treats
Come so quickly then are gone
But the true message that Christmas brings
Will eternally live on

Joy, peace, and goodwill to all
A special gift from God above
To help remind us of Christmastime
And fill our hearts with all Gods love

Christmas a Sacred Day

I love Christmastime
What joy it can truly be
It's filled with warm feelings
That permeates through me

The children are much happier
As Christmas grows so near
They think of all the toys and treats
That magically appear

It is a time of goodwill to all
A time to treasure by far
To look into the darkened night
And see the shining star

What a great event that took place
So many years before
Now we celebrate Christmas
As it makes our spirits soar

For those who know the true meaning
Can fill their hearts with joy
I hope you teach this lesson
To every girl and boy

Enjoy your family traditions
But remember this sacred day
A day we celebrate a special birth
Let us all sing out and pray

Carry You So Far

Fear is a powerful feeling
We all have to face each day
It takes control of what is real
We run when we should stay

Fear should not mean weakness
In so many people's mind
Fear takes a hold and won't let you go
Your courage is so hard to find

You can't run away from all of your fears
No matter what people say
You must turn around and face it
Instead of just running away

You're haunted by things from your past
That scare you for what you might do
You must avoid that wrong path
And trust you will make it through

So face your fears always
Expose them for what they really are
Then show some heart and courage
It will carry you so far

Be on the Right Side

Look to be positive be ready to show
The bright side is better that's where you should go

Beware of the darkness it's always nearby
God's light shines brighter and pierces the eyes

There's a power in being positive in all that you do
Like being an A student helps you in school

Be on the right side and follow the Lord's path
He will keep you safe and away from Satan's wrath

Look at yourself as good not bad
Hold to the rod it will help you feel glad

There is a great power for all of us to see
If we think the right way it will set us free

Believe in the Miracle

Some things happen we can't control
The harder we try the worst things go

It seems so impossible to find the right way
We struggle for answers both night and day

We must believe in the miracle with all of our heart
The Lord has been with us from the start

Great things will happen from the faith that we show
The Lord can work wonders far greater than we know

All we can do is hope for the best
For God will be there to handle the rest

The problems we encounter help us to grow
We learn and become wiser than we ever could know

Each night as I pray I hope that I'll be
A much stronger person who lives to be free

Be Humble and True

Live your life be humble and true
Make the right choices in all that you do

Acknowledge the Lord who helps you each day
And don't be puffed up when it's your turn to pray

Humility is a trait we all must learn
Be willing to help when it is your turn

Don't go on living like you're the only one
Be there for others till your duty is done

Don't fight to be the first one in line
Share what you have and try to be kind

Be quiet as you worship and don't make a scene
Go long without anger and keep your thoughts clean

Beauty Surrounds Us

The children play around the stream
In a land so fresh and green
The mountains stood high and reached for the sky
Their summits could hardly be seen

The trees are tall and rarely fall
The animals run wild and free
The air is clean sweet and pure
A beauty as far as can see

This land we love could soon be gone
The peace and quiet we will miss
And in its place a man made world
All void of loveliness

But now the nature surrounds my soul
And follows me wherever I go
How thankful that God made these wonders to see
And dwell within us for all eternity

Beach

I gaze upon the ocean and hear the wild waves roar
It's such a peaceful feeling to walk along the shore

As I walk about the beach on a clear and sunny day
I sink into another world as my mind is carried away

The seagulls fly so high and soar so gracefully
I feel a thirst for wonder as the magic comes over me

The ocean air is so cool pure and clean
It could never be duplicated by any man-made machine

The wind it blows steady and freely toward the sea
The water goes forever as far as one can see

I want to share this blessing with all I love and know
So they can have the feeling and never let it go

Together we will float along the golden sand
Far away from a reckless world that doesn't understand

Be All You Can

We are on the earth to learn and grow
We try to be all that we can
When tragedy comes we long to know
And pray that we will understand

Losing a loved one can cause enormous pain
We may question why we are even here
The answers may come though they seem in vain
We must trust in the Lord that he cares

People we love will be close by
To comfort our soul as we grieve
We must try to be brave though we want to cry
The hurt is so real that it's hard to believe

We must trust in the Lord as we move along
He will be there close to our side
Don't hold back your tears you've done nothing wrong
Just let him in with your arms open wide

Soak in his love he has saved for you
Be still as he comforts your soul
The one that you love has so much to do
Together your spirits will glow

A Witness From Above

I remember that special day
When Christ was born in a humble way

We sang joyful songs throughout the land
To proclaim to the world the Lord is at hand

We watched our Savior learn and grow
Into a man the whole world will know

Far above we heard him speak
Of loving your neighbor and blessing the meek

The sick were healed the cripple could walk
Thousands would follow him to hear him talk

But so quick his mission was nearing its end
And we knew his great suffering would soon begin

We cried as he wept in the garden that night
As the spear pierced his side it was a sorrowful sight

We watched as they laid him in a tomb cold and gray
But three days quickly passed and the stone rolled away

For God showed his glory in a powerful way
The Son of God has risen on this Easter day

Our Father now reigns with the Lord at his side
Resurrection is a promise to all who will and have died

Autumn or Fall

Something happens in the air each year
The summer breeze begins to get cold
The colors are vivid a wonder to see
The wind becomes stronger and bold

The leaves start to dance
In such a magical way
The trees sway in unison
To create a wonderful ballet

We are the audience
As we gaze with great awe
Mother Nature has named it
Autumn or fall

Apples are falling
As their fruit becomes sweet
They are ripe and so crisp
And are ready to eat

The pumpkins become huge
A sight to be seen
And when they are picked
It's time for Halloween

The nights are longer
The darkness so deep
We seem to get tired more
And enjoy the long sleep

It's so hard to capture
In words to express
What God has created
With such loveliness

I'm glad for the seasons
I give thanks as I pray
We are blessed beyon*d measure*
for every night and each day

A Special and Sacred Time

Christmas is a time when we want our family near
It's a magical time that's filled with holiday cheer

Children start to dream of getting Santa's toys
As the joy of laughter fills every girl and boy

Great things happen on this wonderful day
People are kinder in what they do and say

We try to serve others especially those in need
To give of ourselves as we do our rightly deeds

Christmas is a special and sacred time of year
We learn to help others and relinquish all our fears

If we could emulate the Lord for just a little while
This world that we share would be filled with far less guile

So celebrate his birthday like we always should
Give all you can to others and try to be really good

A Special Gift From Above

Be thankful for your blessings
They're a special gift from above
He's only there to help you
To shower your life with his love

A blessing can be eternal
Far greater than you can compare
You're never completely alone, my friend
The Lord has so much to share

Each morning you take in a breath of fresh air
The dreams from the night now end
A new day is here for the world to see
The adventure of life starts again

The day is done and again you approach night
Did your day go as well as it could
Or was it a day you would like to forget
A day without any good

Blessings come when you need them
Have you learned how to get them to stay
You must count your blessing everyone
Give thanks to the Lord every day

Arms Open Wide

I am a caregiver
I'm someone who cares
When others are gone
I promise to be there

I know it won't be easy
The pain I'll share with you
I hope it will be worth it
In all I want to do

There will be times I feel helpless
When I think I can't endure
I pray that you'll forgive me
My intentions will be pure

I will not stand alone
The Lord is on our side
He will be there when we need him
With his arms open wide

When your journey is over
I know we will meet again
Until that time must come
I'll be with you to the end

Anger Is a Feeling

Anger is a feeling we must endure
It comes and it goes this is for sure

Learning to deal the anger we feel
Is a trait we must conquer for anger is real

Some say that anger can do you some good
Stay in control don't be misunderstood

Learn not to fight every time you are wrong
Say that you're sorry then just move on

Don't let your anger get the best of you
Just swallow your pride and keep your cool

A New Year Will Start

It's Christmastime and there's no need to fear
Look forward to the joy of the upcoming new year

If you are happy when the new year begins
You will have no remorse when the old year ends

What will you do to change the new year
You must erase all your worries and ban all your fears

Are you looking forward to all you can do
Will all of your dreams start to come true

Was last year a good year did everything go right
Or was it filled with the darkness of a cold lonely night

I'm sure there will be surprises as the year moves along
You must keep the faith when something goes wrong

Time never stops no day is the same
If that's not the case it would really be a shame

A New Year Comes

Every time a new year comes
Excitement fills the air
We set our goals the best we can
And try to make them fair

The family gets excited
They know the time is near
Each task they set is a challenge
And failure becomes their fear

Now when the task is finished
They feel the joy of success
This makes them want to shout
And wipe away their stress

A new year brings you victory
A feeling we must know
It drives away the loneliness
And make the heart start to glow

A Medics Call

It's just an old story that I'd like to share
A story of joy and a story of fear
A story told through a young man's eyes
It might make you smile or might make you cry

Deep in the jungle in the middle of war
There's this ninteen year old boy who has been there before
A shout for a medic rings out through the air
The young man gets up and starts to prepare

He knows his duty despite his great fear
To help rescue someone for all lives are dear
He's shot pretty bad what should I do
Then another explosion right next to you

The sting of the metal the burning hot pain
Then in comes another and stings you again
Your weaker now than you were before
You must do something before there is more

I must help my friend but what can I do
Just let out a scream and others will help you
Finally there's someone to take your wounded friend
But sadly they're unable to come out again

Now it's just you you're all on your own
Bleeding and in pain you're all alone
You must make a run for it before it's too late
Your chances are slim but there's no time to wait

A dash through the battle bullets everywhere
Just keep running you might make it there
Finally somewhere to hide so they can't shoot at me
I'm still alive but where could I be

Here comes my rescue a small little man
He carries me to safety as he holds my bloody hand
Now I'm safe from all of this war
My friend heads back into the jungle to look for some more

Alive and Thankful

Some days are good days
Some days are bad
I want to be happy
I want to feel glad

I wish I could remember
Like I used to before
And treasure those moments
That made my heart sing and soar

The names and the faces
I knew everyone
And now there a puzzle
Each memory is gone

I haven't forgotten
How to laugh or to cry
Or say I'm alive and thankful
When someone walks by

Things aren't so bad
They could probably be worse
But I count my blessings
And consider the source

A Great Journey

Dementia is a great journey
Where too many have to go
You can't try to run from it
No matter how much you know

Some say denial is the way
To avoid the pain you endure
Others decide to face it straight on
They hope there might be a cure

It doesn't matter if you're rich or poor
Or have several degrees on the wall
What matters the most is your attitude
Getting up each time that you fall

You can't be afraid of what you might face
The road could feel lonely or cold
Though you are only one of the human race
This is time to be bold

Celebrate survival the best way you can
Remember all the good times you had
So when the dark days come into your path
You won't waste your time feeling sad

A Family With Love

What makes a family to be who they are
If they are united their love will go far

Treat each other the best that they can
Give more than you take learn to understand

Being a father is hard to explain
It's more than the work or the money you gain

A father duty is to protect and provide
Be there when you're needed with arms open wide

A mother is special in so many ways
She nurtures and care for her children each day

When both work together the family does great
The children are happy and each pulls their weight

This seems like a dream that almost could be
But a family with love is a treasure to see

Without Reward

Giving is an act of love
That the Lord would always do
When we give without reward
Our blessings are never through

Where, when, or how we give
Is not as important as why
In giving all that we can in life
It's worth more than money can buy

Everyone needs to help in some way
In doing so our spirits will climb
Helping others who can't help themselves
Is a wise way to spend money, talents and time

You should honor your service
By being as generous as you can
Whatever you give is worth more than you have
There is joy in giving others a helping hand

A Brighter Day

My day is brighter when you come my way
You lighten my burdens and gladden my day

When you are gone I wander about
When you are with me my heart wants to shout

I may not remember all that you do
But the time that we share carries me through

Please stay by my side as much as you can
Your strength we will share as we walk hand in hand

Nine/Eleven

Thousands of Americans died that day
It happened so quickly they were taken away

I was at home watching it all
My body was weak and feeble my mind hit a wall

So many people martyred and slain
We can't let their memories go down in vain

Something snapped inside of me
I need to go back and serve my country

I know I am too old but what could I have done
I'll pray for our warriors that they'll take out everyone

This dishonoring deed made by men far away
Will be avenged I hasten the day

Made in the USA
San Bernardino, CA
01 June 2018